# In Everyone's Shadow

**Theresa Krahenbuhl**

ISBN: 978-1-961392-67-0

# Table Of Contents

# PREFACE

Our story is the journey of an autistic child, who was diagnosed in 1994, at age two and a half. From a mother's perspective, my goal is to inspire hope for others who parent, teach or in some capacity support a child who is neurodiverse. As the saying goes, when you've met one autistic child, you've met one autistic child. There are no two alike and everyone's path is different. Our narrative is testimony to how early diagnosis and intervention, mixed with dedication, love and tolerance are key to helping a child reach their fullest potential.

# Chapter 1. The Beginning

The day I turned seventeen, I left home with no savings, one cardboard box of clothes, a station wagon worth $500, and a part-time after-school job cooking at the local greasy spoon for $1.90 an hour. I was two months into my senior year of high school and was renting the second story of an old clapboard house directly off the downtown square in a small rural Missouri town with barely 1,300 residents.

After shelling out $20 a week for rent, I scraped by on very little, surviving some days on a box of saltine crackers or the lone can of green beans. My substantial calories came from the one free meal I received on the days that I worked at the diner. During those teenage years, the thought of an offspring invoked fear and conjured up images of destitution.

It was then that I realized that I wanted to wait until the age of thirty to start having children. Why thirty? It was a number I pulled out of thin air. Thirty was simply far enough in the future to allow me time to experience life and establish myself financially.

Coasting through senior year, I graduated from high school in May 1979, eventually landing a job in downtown Kansas City, where I balanced the general ledger in the subscription department for a local newspaper.

A year later, I married the football jock that I had dated during my senior year. The marriage was an enormous failure. I had picked a man that was high-spirited and fun, but totally irresponsible. His inability to follow societal rules resulted with him sporadically spending half of our four-year marriage incarcerated in the county jail. And a six-month stay in a state corrections facility. Every other weekend for six months I faithfully drove two and a half hours one way to visit him in jail. I brought his favorite foods to enjoy during each of our visits. He didn't smoke cigarettes but used them to barter for who-knows-what with other inmates. During each visit, I purchased two packs of Marlboros from the vending machine in the visiting room and gave them to him. We kept in touch weekly by writing letters to each other.

My breaking point in the relationship was the day he was released. He did not inform me that he was being discharged. I only discovered that he was released after the fact. I wondered why he kept his impending freedom a secret from me. I soon realized it was because he wanted to be picked up by someone who would bring him a fifth of whiskey. He knew that I would not comply with that request. I was disappointed and disgusted. Alcohol and drugs were the reason he got into trouble. Admittedly, I was overly ready to move on from a lifestyle of one-step-forward-two-steps-back. I promptly consulted with an attorney to end the marriage. Less than thirty minutes at court and I was free to pursue another life.

After huddling over spreadsheets for five years at the local news agency, I was ready for a career change. In 1984, an opportunity to take the Postal Service Exam presented itself and within eight months I was a government employee. That same year I met my second husband, Mike. Mike and I started the very same day at the Postal Service, going through orientation and training together. He was twenty-one and I was twenty-three. After about six months of seeing each other every day at work, we decided to date and eventually married in 1988. We spent our carefree, pre-kid years camping, hiking, skiing the Rockies, boating, swimming, fishing, water skiing, and canoeing spring-fed rivers. We both played softball and volleyball, and attended numerous rock concerts.

By the time I turned thirty, Mike and I had been together for seven years. We had purchased a modest home, and both of us were vested in our jobs. Life was good. Life was uncomplicated. Thinking back to those fun-filled years, if I hadn't set the "have-a-baby-at-thirty" goal, I may have let the child-bearing years pass me by. Although I did not feel a maternal clock ticking, when my third decade crept in, I believed that I was ready to welcome an addition to our family.

As intended, in May 1992, at age thirty, I went into labor with my first son, Alex. I had been admitted to the hospital in the evening and after thirteen exhausting hours of pain and pushing throughout the night with no advancement, it was clear that a cesarean birth was inevitable. Being awake now for over twenty-four fatiguing hours, I was quite relieved to hear that the doctor was finally prepping for late morning surgery.

My mother, who was at my bedside, had the look of any nervous parent before their child heads off to surgery. She gave me a hug and I knew I would be all right. My husband and in-laws also bestowed their well wishes and off I went. Lying flat on the gurney, I watched the fluorescent ceiling lights whisk by as I wheeled through the sanitized halls to surgery. Shortly afterwards my beautiful son Alex entered the world healthy with an Apgar score of nine.

Numb from the waist down and still on the operating table the nurse laid Alex in my arms. His skin was flawless, and to my surprise he had bright blue eyes, which must have been inherited from either my mom or my father-in-law, as Mike and I both have dark brown eyes. I softly spoke to my newborn, but he never looked directly at me. With this being my first child, I thought, "Well, maybe babies don't start connecting until after a few days."

After such a rough-go of birthing, I remained at the hospital for six days. I honestly do not recall the specifics of my health issues and why the doctors kept me so long, I only remember that lovely Demerol drip into my I.V. taking away the pain.

In the following weeks, my precious newborn continued to avert his gaze never making any meaningful eye contact with me. That behavior was an indicator that concerned me. Alex ate well and slept well in those first few months, but the emotional connection to my newborn felt mechanical -- feed, nap, diaper, bathe. We would cuddle on the couch while reading chunky cardboard books with black and white images, and played with numerous infant appropriate toys and rattles, as we enjoyed the soothing sounds of lullaby cassette tapes. When I laid my little guy in his crib for naps, I softly spoke to him while the circulating mobile of pastel-colored, stuffed-fabric horses, bears, and monkeys gently whirred overhead to "Twinkle, Twinkle Little Star." With that said, I felt that there was something missing. I had no recollection of any reciprocal bond between us that would indicate his understanding of my affections.

As months progressed there were numerous signs that led me to believe that something in Alex's development was amiss. The curious symptoms were not familiar to me, so I initially kept my concerns in the back of my mind.

At three months old, I took Alex for his first professional photography shoot. I knew the photographer personally and was confident that she would do a great job. The dear girl struggled to get Alex to look at her with any reaction. We were hopeful for a smile, but she could not elicit any emotional response. She pulled out all the stops...the floppy stuffed bunny, the squeaky mouse, the goofy faces and antics, the baby talk. Feeling somewhat embarrassed for her as she worked tirelessly for an hour, the best we came away with was a few shots consisting of a blank stare.

At six months, I took Alex to a different professional photographer, hopeful to get a cheerful Christmas photo. He was dressed in a festive red, onesie along with a matching Santa hat. Again, there was no emotional connection made throughout the picture taking process. I was weary, but still had no idea that this type of behavior was a red flag for a serious condition. At nine months, the professional picture taking process continued to be an agonizing event. At that point I determined that I would not put yet another photographer through the struggle of trying to get Alex's attention, let alone a meaningful smile. So, the nine-month-old picture was the last attempt to gain a professional photo for at least a year.

At ongoing pediatric visits, I measured my baby's progress closely against the range of typically developing milestones that were provided by the doctor. Alex seemed to be a little behind the norm with motor skills, but nothing drastic. He sat unsupported at seven months and crawled at eight months. He started walking at thirteen months, perhaps a little late. His very first tooth did not emerge until twelve months of age. Although his development targets were reached at the far end of the scale, I was assured by professionals that there was no reason for alarm. With no robust internet in 1993 I naively accepted their complacency.

When Alex turned one, we held a birthday party at a child-friendly fast-food establishment for family and friends. The assigned hostess of the party was a bubbly, patient teenage girl who tried to get Alex to play a game. He was asked to throw a small, red plastic ball into a free-standing open paper bag on the floor directly in front of him. A simple task for a one-year-old. The teenager repeatedly modeled the game for Alex, but he never grasped what was being asked of him. The other children were standing in line and eager to play so I picked up Alex and directed his attention to the toddlers who were now engaged in the activity. I wondered if he merely needed a little more time to process the game. Throughout the exercise he showed zero interest and never participated. Again, my concern for his lack of connection, along with his inability to follow direction was mentally filed away.

The day I gave Alex his first haircut at eighteen months old was another incident of unusual behavior that puzzled me. I sat him in his highchair, inserted an animated classic into the VCR, and grabbed my shears. At the time, "101 Dalmatians" was one of his favorite videos. All throughout the cutting he was fidgety, and I accidentally clipped the back of his upper ear with the scissors. The small puncture resulted in a tiny drop of blood. Curiously, Alex did not cry. Without intention, his tiny hand brushed his ear never taking his focus from the TV. He knew something had happened but did not give it a second thought. He displayed no pain and there were no tears. I was mortified for drawing blood and perplexed that nicking him drew no painful response.

At Alex's eighteen-month routine checkup, I expressed my concerns to his pediatrician. According to the language milestones chart provided by the physician, Alex should have been using at least twenty words. He used two...baby and da-da. I mentioned his lack of verbalization to the doctor, along with my growing concern for Alex's inability to follow directions or to communicate his wants and needs. I said to her, "His lack of social connecting is starting to result with frustration for him and is leading to emotional meltdowns."

The doctor calmly said, "Well sometimes children just don't have anything to say. He'll eventually start talking."

Feeling slightly offended, I immediately thought to myself that her statement was unfairly dismissive. I came to the realization that this pediatrician was not going to be able to address my worries that had been building over the last year and a half. But again, without well-developed internet in the '90s I did not know where to turn. My only option at that point was to find another pediatrician, which is what I did.

Moments of confusion and frustration continued with Alex. At age two his language skills seemed to regress, and he no longer used any words. He would grunt, squeal, and make unintelligible noises. I recall one exhausting dinner out at a restaurant. Alex started to fuss, motioning as if he wanted something that was on the table. Mike and I offered him everything within sight from the saltshaker to a spoon, to crackers, to toys, to the plastic flower centerpiece, attempting to get a positive response, but he refused everything. His irritation grew, and he cried louder making an embarrassing scene. We were exasperated and disheartened that we never figured out what he wanted. Thankfully, our food arrived, and we were able to redirect him with the animation of dancing, dinosaur-shaped chicken nuggets.

At a subsequent doctor visit with Alex's new pediatrician, I relayed my concerns for his lack of words and difficult behavior. The new Pediatrician suggested that I make an appointment with a Speech and Language Pathologist at North Kansas City Hospital for an evaluation. I thought, "Finally, I have some actionable guidance!"

A phone call later, we were on the books for an appointment at the hospital, scheduled for the following week. As a result of that evaluation, the Speech and Language Pathologist documented a delay in Alex's language skills of approximately twenty months. Her report stated that at age two, children should possess a vocabulary of approximately 300 words and utilize two-word sentences dynamically. Throughout the therapist's evaluation, Alex adamantly refused to separate from me, and was mostly uncooperative to her commands. His only discernable word uttered during the evaluation sounded like "Hi."

As a next step, she suggested that we have Alex's hearing tested. I then made an appointment with Children's Mercy Hospital for a hearing assessment.

After checking in at Children's Mercy, the gentleman assigned to conduct the hearing evaluation placed Alex and me in a sound-proof booth. Alex was sitting on my lap facing forward. The booth was quiet and dark with dim lighting. Then suddenly, a small, stuffed monkey to our right, began crashing hand-held cymbals. Alex immediately looked to the right. When another object on the left made a noise, Alex looked to the left. There were high and low-pitched noises coming from the upper and lower corners of the booth. Each time a sound was presented, Alex appropriately turned in the direction of the noise. After the twenty-minute test concluded, I was relieved that

Alex's hearing was diagnosed as normal, but I still did not have answers regarding his delayed development.

With normal hearing but delayed speech, the Children's Mercy staff recommended intensive early language intervention for Alex. I learned through additional conversation with the hospital staff, that the county health center near my residence mercifully offered therapy sessions at no cost to the parent. With a hopeful outlook, I placed Alex on a six-month waiting list for speech and language therapy.

Five months had passed when I received a long-awaited call from the county health center, and at age two and a half, Alex started speech therapy. We entered a room that had a large fish tank, some toys, a small round child-sized table, and a few child-sized chairs. The floor was dingy white tile, and the walls were a bright, white-washed cinder block. There were no windows, as to avoid any unnecessary distractions.

I was able to observe each session because Alex refused to separate from me. I stuffed myself into a child-sized chair and cringed as I watched the energetic speech therapist painfully struggle to obtain from Alex an appropriate response to her questions. "What is this?" she asked as she held up a toy car. Next, she asked "Where are the fish?" holding her hands up and outward. "Who is this?" she asked while pointing to me. She was young and very patient, continuously asking him questions and getting no response. Alex was non-compliant to her every request. When the therapist pursued a little more aggressively, he became more aggravated. Now screaming and crying, Alex crawled under the table on hands and knees displaying his usual meltdown behavior that occurred when he was pressured to engage in an activity that required his response.

During ongoing therapy sessions, Alex seemingly ignored the therapist and stared at the fish tank. At one point she squatted down to his level and got physically close. He did not want her near him, and I could tell that he was close to another sensory-overload episode. I mumbled to myself, "Oh no, here comes the notorious meltdown." After she repeatedly implored him for a response and realized she was getting nowhere, she said to Alex, "Just tell me to stop." I could see that he was digesting her comment. He never spoke the word stop, but he did physically push her away with the gentleness of one hand.

Leaving the health center that day, the speech therapist recommended that I require Alex to walk up the outside concrete steps that led to the parking lot by himself, versus me carrying him. In other words, do not give in or pick him up if he cries, get him to follow my commands. He was just a small toddler and there were about fifteen, steep concrete steps.

With alternating hands and feet, he screamed and cried at each step for what seemed like an excruciating half hour, as I sat at the top of the stairs encouraging him to take one step at a time. He had successfully taken about ten steps during that lengthy heart-wrenching meltdown, until it was clear to me that he was at an impasse. I felt that if I let the torturous screaming go on any longer it would border on abuse, so I picked him up, gave him a big hug, congratulated him for the ten steps conquered and headed for the car saddened and frustrated. The step exercise was never addressed at our following session, so I can only assume that the therapist was watching from a window and took note of the outcome.

Alex attended twelve arduous speech therapy sessions over a period of about six weeks with no measurable progress. Understanding that her patient was not advancing, the therapist suggested that I take Alex to the Kansas City Regional Office (KCRO). I had no idea what KCRO was or what they did. I didn't even know what questions to ask, but I dutifully made the appointment and scheduled half a day off work.

When appointment day came, I dressed and fed Alex, then left the house by 8:00 am for the Regional Office in downtown Kansas City. When we arrived, I was informed that a team of professionals would evaluate Alex, although I had no clue what they were looking for. The team consisted of a Registered Nurse, a Psychologist, a Speech Pathologist, and a Registered Occupational Therapist (OTR).

Alex and I were escorted to a small room that resembled a doctor's office. I remember the nurse asking me to describe Alex's current behavior. Among his lack of language and varying degrees of meltdowns, I also conveyed that in Alex's frustrated moments he would head butt me in the legs. After some additional conversation with the team, testing began.

Again, Alex was totally non-compliant and refused any interaction. With Alex sitting on my lap facing away from me the OTR rang a small porcelain bell. I thought that was an odd thing to do since I had already told them that Alex had successfully completed a hearing test. I could not see Alex's facial reaction to the bell, as he was facing forward, however I was informed that they were watching for Alex's reaction to the sharply ringing noise. According to the professionals, instead of grabbing for the bell as most typically developing children would, his body language suggested that the noise was painful to his ears. At one point the porcelain bell was extended for Alex to take, and he frantically shook his head and jabbered what sounded like "no-no-no."

As the evaluation proceeded and with Alex still on my lap, the psychologist handed me a small, green, cloth covered box about three inches squared with a miniature toy inside. The psychologist asked, "Can you get Alex to open the lid of the box?" I tried many times to entice him, at one point even opening and closing the lid very quickly in front of him so that he could briefly see the toy inside. He showed no interest. After about ten minutes of trying to engage him, we agreed to stop the exercise. Alex never reached for the box.

The team of professionals took Alex into a separate room, as I waited alone for about an hour. As noted in the evaluation report, Alex frequently screamed, cried, or just generally fussed when someone talked to him, requested that he perform a task, or casually looked at him. By now, the evaluation was well into three strenuous hours.

After testing was completed, one of the female professionals met with me while the rest of the team kept Alex entertained in a separate room. She calmly explained to me that the team had concluded a diagnosis of Moderate Autism. She continued through the summarized evaluation line by line, pointing out fifteen specific characteristics that distinguish children with Autism from other developmentally delayed, behavioral disordered, or emotionally disturbed children. Those markers were:

1. Relating to People
2. Imitation
3. Emotional Response
4. Body Use
5. Object Use
6. Adaptation to Change
7. Visual Response
8. Listening Response
9. Taste, Smell and Touch (Response and Use)
10. Fear or Nervousness
11. Verbal Communication
12. Nonverbal Communication
13. Activity Level
14. Level and Consistency of Intellectual Response
15. General Impressions

At this point my head was spinning, trying to make sense of what I was hearing. All I could think was, "What the heck is Autism?" It was the first time I had heard the word. I fought to hold back tears, as I attempted to process the information and understand what this diagnosis meant for my child's future. I felt overwhelmed, deflated, and hollow inside. In hindsight, I should have never gone to this appointment alone.

So, what is Autism? The following is a paragraph from a publication by the National Institute of Mental Health – Decade of the Brain.

*"Isolated in worlds of their own, people with Autism appear indifferent and remote and are unable to form emotional bonds with others. Although people with this baffling brain disorder can display a wide range of symptoms and disability, many are incapable of understanding other people's thoughts, feelings, and needs. Often, language and intelligence fail to develop fully, making communication and social relationships difficult. Some people with Autism engage in repetitive activities, like rocking or banging their heads, or rigidly following familiar patterns in their everyday routines. Some are painfully sensitive to sounds, touch, sight, or smell."*

It would have been extremely helpful if I had been given a little heads up on what the Kansas City Regional Office evaluation entailed and the potential outcome. Receiving this type of news is too serious to be blindsided. Only afterwards did I learn that the Kansas City Regional Office was a unit established by the Missouri Department of Mental Health. Having experienced the delivery of traumatic news with no other family present, I would highly recommend that an adult accompany the parent/caregiver to any child's evaluation. Not only for emotional support, but to help absorb the assessment results. After that blow, the information being conveyed to me was glossing over in my disoriented brain, as if listening to Charlie Brown's teacher.

My only saving grace that morning was the Case Manager that was assigned to Alex before we left. She carefully explained that she would visit our home periodically to ensure that Alex had access to resources that would help him excel developmentally. I left with a small ray of hope, but still struggling to make sense of an Autism diagnosis. Today, Autism is widely recognized and there is a plethora of accessible information compared to what little was available in 1994.

Still reeling from just receiving the diagnosis bombshell, I drove Alex to his babysitter, a kind, gray-haired, older woman who watched a few other children in her home with the assistance of her adult daughter. I informed her of the news, and the blank look on her face told me that she knew as much about Autism as I did. From there, I robotically drove to work. I had no clear direction as to what I should be doing next to help Alex, so I went to work where I was knowledgeable and comfortable. Being there gave me some semblance of emotional control.

After about a month of feeling disconnected, confused, and emotionally crushed, I had a moment of clarity for next steps. Had I not been blindsided, learning that my son had a disability may have been easier to process. I was currently working very long hours for the Postal Service and attending community college. I had finally come to the realization that my college days were over. Instead, I would need to focus all my energy on understanding where to find the services and supports to ensure Alex's success at navigating his world. Clearly, I did not possess the knowledge or special skills to teach him.

I immediately became active in the Autism community and strived to learn as much as I could. I joined a monthly Autism support group held at a local church. The group consisted of parents and professionals. There were guest speakers each month. Some guests provided knowledge of Autism diagnoses and its vast spectrum of conditions. Some guests promoted their intended solution to Autism whether it be vitamins, chelation, Applied Behavior Analysis (ABA) therapy, enzymes, prescription drugs, gluten-free/casein-free diets, food allergy analyses, etc. As a parent of a child with a developmental disability, one may be inclined to try anything and everything with the desperate hope of finding a cure. I will share this very valuable piece of advice I was given early on by a Special Education teacher that I greatly respected..."*Be CAUTIOUS, as there are many possible treatments to alleviate the symptoms of Autism…REALIZE, there is no documented cure.*"

As the mother of an autistic child, I would highly recommend that when a parent obtains an Autism diagnosis, they immediately get involved in an Autism support group. The wealth of knowledge presented is a treasure trove. This type of forum can provide emotional support, alert you to the school districts that provide the best advocates (or not), identify doctors that work well with Autistic patients, and educate on how to access federal, state, and county funding for resources; just to name a few. Additionally, connecting with parents and professionals that handle children on the Autism spectrum has the potential to ease your stress by knowing that you are not alone. Listening to someone else's woeful story of their child's uncontrollable behaviors can make you grateful that at least *today*, it's not your struggle.

Social media makes joining an Autism support group far easier than it was in the nineties. There are fabulous local online support groups available and regional chapters of non-profit, Autism focused agencies. Your child's Case Manager (typically assigned because of diagnosis) or Service Provider (hired professional help either personally or publicly funded) should be able to provide direction.

After the crushing Autism diagnosis, I continued to remain employed by the Postal Service. With ten years already invested in the company, I thought it would be unwise to relinquish my pension and no longer contribute to my retirement account. Visions of my son living under a bridge as an adult haunted me and constantly motivated me to achieve financial stability. Throughout my thirty-four years at the Postal Service, I was blessed to have advanced in my career, allowing me to establish and fund a special needs trust. In Alex's early years my biggest fear was, "What would happen to him once Mike and I were gone?"

No doubt about it, having to be at work at 7:00 a.m. was truly dreadful. I am not a morning person and I've never had a cup of coffee in my life. The alarm would jar me awake at 5:30 a.m. After hitting the snooze button as many times as I could get away with, I'd stumble into the shower and finally achieve consciousness. Hastily, I tried to make myself as presentable as possible, although the Postal facility where I worked was in an underground cave complex, so the effort was minimal. Hurrying to wake my infant from his crib, I would change and dress him, make a bottle, strap him into the baby carrier that doubled as a car seat and propped his bottle to feed him breakfast before heading to the babysitter. Every morning I felt like I was feverishly moving in double time. And forget about breakfast, that was never an option. One morning I was cruising at my usual hurried pace. I had already loaded my car the previous night with the diaper bag stuffed with fresh diapers, clean clothes, and formula. Dashing my way to the garage, I quickly lifted the baby carrier from the hard wood floor and catapulted my young son into a face plant. I was horrified!! Unknowingly I had forgotten to strap Alex in the car carrier. He briefly cried as I cuddled and comforted him. Thankfully, he was not seriously hurt, but my stomach roiled all day at my stupidity and carelessness.

As the hectic days and months passed, it was evident that my current pace of life needed some adjustment. I was presently taking a college course and working for a Postal facility that *mandated* a 56-hour work week. I worked ten-hour days Monday through Thursday, eight hours on Friday and eight hours on Saturday with no flexibility. For those of you who have worked in labor for the government, I'm sure you can relate to the rigidity of hitting a timeclock and needing a doctor's excuse for any absence over two days in length. After four long years of enduring the overtime insanity, I thought enough is enough! Alex had recently been diagnosed and I knew I needed to devote my time to family. I pondered, "How am I going to get out of working mandated overtime?" Afterall, I was conditioned to be a rule follower.

After a few days of contemplation, I called the Kansas City Regional Office, explained my situation, and asked if they would be so kind as to write a letter on my behalf. The following memo was printed on KCRO letterhead, written by Alex's evaluating Psychologist and mailed directly to the Director of my employment facility.

*"As requested by Theresa Krahenbuhl, I am writing this letter regarding her son Alex who was evaluated by this agency on November 29, 1994. At that time Alex was administered numerous tests, and an extensive*

*review of his developmental and behavioral history was conducted by me. After spending the morning with Theresa and Alex it was determined that Alex met the criteria as having Autistic Disorder.*

*Autism is a behavioral syndrome that is characterized by many atypical and inappropriate developmental responses which is present from birth. Because of the atypical and all-encompassing nature of an Autistic child's responses to his environment, specialized early intervention services in a consistent, structured setting, is a key component in that child developing to his full potential. To achieve this goal, it is very important that an Autistic child's family be involved in all aspects of the early intervention process at home, school, and the community which at times can be almost overwhelming.*

*Therefore, it would be beneficial to Alex's development if his mother, Theresa could be allowed some flexibility in her working hours that would enable her to effectively participate in programming and meet his special needs."*

When the Director received the letter, he came to my department and personally expressed his sincere apologies. I was floored! Working in labor for the Postal Service had been a militaristic experience to this point. Not that I expected him to be a jerk, but I did not anticipate that the letter would be met with any amount of compassion, especially when the facility had an abundance of work that needed extra effort from its personnel. Management surely had to be under great stress to fill the enormous backlog of stamp orders in a timely fashion. As my discussion with the Director continued, I clarified that the letter meant that I would no longer be available to work overtime, and he candidly said, "Okay." And that was that. No more overtime. No more squeezing grocery shopping, laundry, and family commitments into one day off. Relief flooded my entire being. That moment also marked my last semester as a college student.

# Chapter 2. The Lighthouse

With our newfound Autism diagnosis, Alex's Case Manager informed me that he was eligible to participate in Missouri's early intervention program called First Steps. The First Steps program was administered by The Lighthouse, a special needs preschool. On January 3, 1995, at age two and a half and still wordless, I took Alex by the hand and excitedly walked him into the preschool to participate in his first day of full-time learning. I was feeling very optimistic that this special place would start the process of helping Alex to effectively communicate, therefore reducing his frustration. Three goals were identified and documented in his personal plan:

1. Consistent oral motor exercises - *typically accomplished with a variety of textures and flavors at lunch and snack time*

2. Consistent imitation of expressive vocabulary

3. Obtain eye contact in response to cue "look at me"

At the end of his first day, I was delightfully encouraged to learn that I would be receiving daily hand-written reports that outlined the day's activities, associated behaviors (good and bad) and any progress. The report was broken down into:

- Gross Motor Skills – throwing, catching, marching, jumping, kicking, biking

- Fine Motor Skills – puzzles, Legos, barrel of monkeys, peg boards

- Art Activities – coloring, glue, glitter, scissors, string

- Nap Time

- Circle Time – daily weather, stories, fingerplays, songs

- Small Groups – animal sounds, colors, body parts

- Toileting Notes – along with a weekly potty chart breaking down wet/dry by the hour

- Lunch and Snack Notes – what was served vs. what was consumed, mastering utensils

- Personal notes from each of the three female professionals that aided Alex daily

Each day there were different and engaging activities. Time was spent hitting and retrieving little plastic golf balls, listening to music and identifying instruments, making footprints in the snow, assembling doughnut bird feeders, playing with shaving cream, paint, and playdoh, stringing beads, scooping rice and pasta, and waterplay.

With all the fun play activity and absence of actual letter learning, perhaps a parent may wonder how their developmentally delayed child will catch up with their typically developing peers. In a 1989 "Kansas City Parent" article written by Sue Carpenter, Executive Director of the Johnson County Child Care Association, she states:

*Experts affirm that children learn best through a hands-on, play-oriented approach. For instance, coloring books and worksheets teach children that there is one right way to complete a task. On the other hand, by providing children with paints and paper, they can explore all the possibilities of what can be done with the materials. They might discover that runny paint drips faster than thick paint. Or that red paint mixed with blue paint makes purple. By using these materials frequently, the child develops muscle control, a sense of mastery, and the joy of creativity. In short, the best pre-reading materials are not letters and worksheets, but blocks, paints, and puzzles.*

*Alex, painting at home.*

In addition to all the fun learning activities, Alex had thirty minutes each day devoted to one-on-one speech therapy. The therapist immediately went to work on Alex's speech deficit by teaching him sign language. This was (and still is in some cases) a successful method for moving a non-verbal child from silence and frustration to verbalization and meaningful communication. The speech therapist provided a separate hand-written note each day outlining what she and Alex had tackled. If there had been any resistance from Alex during a session, that behavior was identified.

Transitioning to speech therapy was by far the toughest part of Alex's day. When he was taken from the classroom to the therapy room, he would cry, refuse to walk, stiffen his body when being carried, and blow his nose. As Alex became accustomed to the routine, those behaviors were eliminated. If Alex was not compliant during a therapy session, items were temptingly dangled as an incentive, such as crackers, hot wheels, or bubbles. Those items were withheld until he cooperated. Initially, a lot of time was spent on the floor crying, but he eventually learned the concept of rewards. Thinking back, if I had had a piece of candy in my hand when I tried to get Alex to climb the concrete steps at the speech therapy office, I may have achieved better results. But my upbringing did not include bribery, so I was unaware of such a concept.

Another difficulty during Alex's school day was transitioning from "free-play" to Circle Time, where the group worked on sensory integration.

Circle Time was structured, requiring his full attention and participation. Sometimes, it was necessary to physically move him to this group. He would cry for several minutes, but finally come around and chug his little arms to "Wheels on the Bus" or *put his right foot in, put his right foot out, put his right foot in and shake it all about.*

Knowing what went well throughout Alex's day and what behaviors were a struggle allowed me to understand what needed reinforcement at home. The teacher's daily comments were always inspiring and written with a positive outlook even if they had experienced negative behaviors. I could not have been more pleased with the Lighthouse staff. As the weeks passed, Alex showed an improved understanding of new concepts and increasingly was able to follow more directions.

My mother-in-law was one of the sweetest, friendliest, and most loving people that I have had the privilege of knowing. I have nothing but fond memories of her beautiful smile and kindness. When each of her three boys were born, she provided them with security blankets. When her little guys outgrew their attachment to the soft, silky comfort, she carefully stowed them in a cedar chest in the attic.

Naturally, when Alex was born, she retrieved my husband's baby blanket from the attic. It was a pale yellow, silky, quilted blanket with a yellow satin trim. Suffice to say, Alex became very attached to that blanket, with it rarely leaving his sight.

Eventually, it became so ragged from continuous washings that I had to sew on a new satin trim. In hindsight, that would have been the perfect opportunity to permanently separate Alex from his blanket, but with working full time, running a household, and trying to understand my child's needs there was no foresight. I was purely surviving in the moment.

The first morning that Alex arrived at the Lighthouse Preschool, the blanket was in tow. Alas, the Lighthouse staff had a different view of the coveted dependence. Unfortunately, I had not possessed the intuition that Alex's blanket addiction would provide a distraction in a learning environment. Consequently, on that first morning the teacher instructed my two-and-a-half-year-old to leave the blanket in his cubby, along with his backpack filled with pullups, wipes, extra clothes, snacks, and sunscreen.

You can imagine how the attempted blanket separation went. Streaming tears, escalated wailing, and lots of horizontal floor time.

When I walked into the preschool later that afternoon to take Alex home, the teaching staff clued me in and asked that I support their request to start the blanket-weaning process. I realized that it was necessary if Alex was going to learn how to follow directions, but I knew it would not be easy for either of us. Knowing that his comfort would be stripped at the tender age of two and a half pulled on my heart strings. The transition of blanket-weaning at school took a few tearful weeks. To facilitate the process, the preschool staff suggested that I cut a small square from the blanket that Alex could keep in his pants pocket. Surprisingly, he did not balk when offered the tiny cloth remnant in lieu of the entire anxiety-reducing fabric, and apparently, he was comforted knowing that a piece of security was close at hand. Eventually Alex succumbed to the classroom routine without toting around a distracting object, and in time successfully learned to disregard the small scrap of material. The teaching staff always provided positive reinforcement and Alex gained a sense of pride when he mastered a new skill.

Now that my toddler was fully engaged in his new learning environment, the time had arrived for me to enhance my knowledge and understanding of Autism. I had recently learned that the Kansas City Regional Office was aligned with the Northwest Missouri Autism Project, a family support services program that had been established in November 1993, just one year prior to Alex's diagnosis. The Autism Project's philosophy was to provide training, consultation, and direct services and supports to families based on behavioral issues identified in the home, at school, or in the community. They also offered advocacy assistance related to the child's educational needs in their current school placement.

With the growing number of Autism diagnoses, the Autism Project was already maintaining a waiting list of two to six months for occupational therapy, in-home behavioral supports, language-communication therapy, and other intensive early interventions that were vital to Alex's emotional and behavioral growth. Part of the delay was the inability to locate qualified service-provider personnel. I could certainly understand that dilemma. Based on anecdotes that kept coming up in conversation with therapists and Case Managers, working with special needs children was a strenuous job and the pay did not reflect the effort that was required.

Throughout the next year I attended educational parent workshops and motivational Autism symposiums where attendance was funded by the Autism Project. One memorable event was watching Temple Grandin, an autistic adult, walk on stage with only socks on her feet, to give her life's testimonial. An audience member to my right whispered in my ear that Temple had sensory issues related to speaking in front of an audience and could not tolerate shoes during her presentation. I cannot swear to the accuracy of that statement. Nonetheless, Temple was fearlessly standing on stage at the podium with no shoes on her feet. She did a marvelous job explaining how she developed equipment that promoted the humane treatment of livestock for slaughter. Listening to her intelligently speak about her engineering success, in her somewhat monotone voice, with her robotic verbal cadence, was such an inspiration! I left the auditorium feeling enlightened and hopeful that Alex's future could possibly hold personal fulfillment.

When I look back on the timing of Alex's diagnosis, I feel so very fortunate that he had access to the Autism Project program in its infancy. Over the years, I frequently heard parents of autistic children complain about being on the Autism Project waiting list for several years, as sadly, government funding for this crucially beneficial program did not keep up with demand. To be required to pay for every Autism related service out of pocket would surely have caused our family great financial strain, adding to the emotional stress that comes with raising a child with developmental delays.

# Chapter 3. Early Childhood Education

At age three Alex became eligible to enroll in Early Childhood Education services through the North Kansas City School District; a public institution. Small group instruction was identified by school personnel as necessary for Alex to acquire skills specified in his documented education plan. Unique factors defined in the plan for improvement were:

- Social capability
- Appropriate interaction with others
- Use of clear language
- Appropriate behaviors
- Adaptability to environment

The Early Childhood Education program was only four hours each day which meant that my little man would have to ride the enormous, full-sized yellow school bus from the Lighthouse preschool, traveling eight miles to the Early Education Center and then eight miles back to the Lighthouse. There was an attendant on the bus to assist with the three or four children that were in transport. I never received any negative feedback on bus behavior, so yay! That was one transition that went smoothly. Progress!

Although Alex's fine motor skills continued to show a slight delay, communication and socialization continued to be a deficit. This was especially noted during testing when the measurement of cognitive function required a verbal response. At times Alex could echo partial words like "tee" for teeth or "doe" for "door." Other times, his babbling was unintelligible. He had very minimal usage of two-word utterances, like "all done" and "want juice." His struggle with communication continued to provoke uncooperative behaviors.

Most days, the transition from the gross motor play area to speech therapy sparked resistance by Alex. His anxiety rose knowing that he was moving from unstructured playtime in the gym to a classroom environment that required his intellectual response. Subsequently, the change in activity required physical intervention by his therapist, Miss Anita. After Miss Anita physically carried an obstinate, squirming, kicking, and crying Alex into the small therapy room, he immediately crawled under the desk chair. He remained huddled in a ball, with his head, knees, and elbows supported on the carpet. When Miss Anita removed the chair, Alex went further under the desk and continued with his meltdown. He remained there while Miss Anita gave him time to gather his emotions and then she cleverly offered him a miniature toy truck. The distraction of receiving a toy that he enjoyed helped Alex to calm his anxiety and Miss Anita could then ease him into the therapy session. Miss Anita had the patience of a saint and the gritty determination of an elite athlete.

Sensory issues persisted for Alex at school. He expressed discomfort to bright lights and was content to be in the dark. A dark calming tent within the classroom setting was used when Alex, as well as other students were in sensory overload. When he could not successfully transition from one task to another, tantrums ensued. He would then climb into the dark tent and allow his senses to calm so that he could regain his composure.

Sound was also a catalyst for challenging behaviors. After the first haircut debacle with a clipped ear, I was hesitant to cut Alex's hair myself. I found a barber who was happy to give my toddler a cut. The friendly, stocky, white-haired, older man with a buzz cut sat Alex in the big swivel chair and wrapped the barber's cape around him. So far so good. The barber carefully chopped away with his scissors, but when the electric shaver started up, Alex went nuts. He screamed at the top of his lungs, ducking the vibrating shaver every time the frightening device got close to his head. The barber softly told Alex that the shaver would not hurt him and placed the running electric device on his own hand to show that it was harmless.

The screaming and dodging continued with each attempt to get the shaver near his head. After about twenty desperate minutes of me, Mike and the barber pleading for cooperation and getting nowhere, I finally sat in the chair with Alex on my lap. I wrapped my arms tightly around his little trembling body restricting his arms like a straitjacket and used all my strength to keep his teeth from sinking into my arm, allowing the barber to finish the job. The tension between my child in sensory overload and the ex-marine who wanted to get the job done was stressful. The result was a choppy looking haircut, but at least his bangs were out of his eyes. Depleted of my strength, I weakly murmured, "Oh my god, we can't go through this trauma every time my kid needs a cut!"

After consulting with Alex's support team and engaging in many discussions with other parents of autistic children, we suspected that the intense buzzing of the vibrating shears was piercingly magnified in Alex's ears, causing severe pain and fright. Our suspicion of sound sensitivity was proven when we found a hair salon about forty-five miles from our home that specifically catered to little ones and did not use electric razors. The stylists performed their artistry with scissors and were masters of distraction, successfully coaxing Alex to remain in the chair. The salon offered a few activity centers with interactive toys. They encouraged early arrival so that the youngsters could spend time playing before their scheduled appointment, allowing them to acclimate to their surroundings. Additionally, the salon had an abundance of candy for purchase that worked perfectly well with bribing Alex into submission.

As we had hoped, Alex had no sensory episodes at this kid-friendly salon and received a decent haircut albeit a little more costly than a barber. The salon was only open during the week until 7:00 pm.

But the lengthy hour drive across town was well worth the extra cost and added pressure of leaving work at 3:30 pm, racing twenty-five minutes to the preschool, transitioning Alex to the car, then fighting rush hour traffic through the heart of the city, to arrive at the salon in time to start the entire haircut process. This ritual occurred about every six weeks for many years until Alex became accustomed to a salon setting. Eventually we transferred to a generic salon closer to home. As he aged into his teen years, he could tolerate the buzz of the barber's electric shaver and to this day, Alex patronizes the same barber that he befriended while in high school. More progress!

During preschool Alex was slowly relating to his three-year-old peers, however there were still signs at home that showed his disinterest to engage in play with other children. He generally preferred to play alone, either lining up his Hot Wheels or painting or drawing. One mild, sunny day our extended family was visiting a local park. The birds were singing, and the squirrels were scurrying up and down an enormous oak tree playing a game of tag. Alex's two male cousins who were in his age range, were visiting the park with us. I was blowing soap bubbles as my little nephews were squealing, chasing, and popping the floating spheres. Alex was sitting on a nearby blanket, laughing and clapping, content to watch his cousins have a great time. I said, "Come on Alex, join us and pop some bubbles." He never acknowledged that I was speaking to him. He just sat there immensely enjoying the show. At that age, most children would prefer being engaged in the activity versus sitting on the sidelines. Alex's gait and gross motor coordination was still a little awkward. He may not have been able to keep up with his athletic cousins. Or lacking a competitive nature, maybe he was more comfortable as an observer. Possibly the excited squealing was too intense for his ears. Without clear communication, I could not determine with certainty why he did not participate.

I was clear on one thing. Early intervention was an absolute blessing and vital to Alex's progression. Remember two years earlier during his initial evaluation, when he was unable to follow verbal instructions to retrieve a toy from inside a small box? Now, during routine cognitive testing he was able to find an object hidden under a container, among many other simple tasks, by following verbal instruction. More encouraging progress!

Socialization and play skills were greatly improving. Alex could interact appropriately with peers and tolerate them within his play space. He could take turns in play when an adult was close by to help structure the play. If unattended, Alex would still take a toy from a peer and run. Strategies that were helpful with teaching Alex how to share toys included asking him to hold his hand out and ask, "My turn?"

Initially Alex used a picture schedule to help him understand and make transitions throughout the Early Education school day. The visual schedule was discontinued after six months when he successfully demonstrated an understanding of his daily routine.

By the end of Early Childhood Education Alex was turning age five. He now used sentences of three to four words, participated in activities when motivated, mostly stayed with his peers in group activities, asked simple questions, spontaneously offered comments, cheerfully greeted others, was independent in toileting at school and fully understood the routine of his day.

# Chapter 4. Elementary School

After two promising years of growth in Early Childhood Education, Alex was moving on to kindergarten. Although he was attending a regular elementary school, he was assigned to a self-contained classroom with a handful of other developmentally delayed children. He had slowly improved his coping and learning skills, but still had some unacceptable school related behaviors and deficiencies in language.

His new teacher Ms. Christine, along with his previous teachers identified significant areas for behavioral improvement:

- Poor attention
- Self-control
- Excessive resistance

The team of teachers drafted a remarkable Individual Education Plan (IEP) specifically written to address Alex's developmental and educational needs. Typically, the IEP document is a collaborative activity between parents and the school, however in his early education years I did not experience Alex's unusual behaviors when pressured to conform at school, so I initially let the experts take the reins on the IEP content. The goals were meticulously documented and aligned with evaluation criteria, evaluation procedures, review dates and the anticipated end results.

The new plan required this five-year-old to:

- Stay in a group setting until he had permission to leave
- Wait to take his turn while playing a game with peers

- Take turns being a line leader without pouting, pushing, and raging

- Obtain permission to take personal items that belonged to others

- Return items that have been loaned to him without running away and hiding them

- Improve expressive and receptive language:

  - Stay on topic when asked to discuss a specific subject *(without changing the subject to dinosaurs – his favorite)*

  - Express self effectively

  - Follow multi-step directions given orally

  - Respond to detailed questions related to a story read to him

  - Identify vocabulary meaning through listening

  - Identify answers to "wh" questions (who, what, why, where, when)

  - Revise own ungrammatical sentences

  - Define vocabulary by function, description, definition, and synonym

  - Respond appropriately to another person's use of homonyms, idioms, and analogies

A lofty agenda by any standards! Especially when the special education teacher had more than one special-needs child and they all had varying degrees of disability, presenting different strengths, weaknesses, and needs.

On a hot August day in 1997, Alex started kindergarten with his new special education teacher, Ms. Christine. Ms. Christine was a very high energy, middle-aged woman who exuded an enormous amount of dedication. In her "welcome to my classroom" letter she provided her home phone number in case parents had any questions after hours. Her *home* phone! Who does that? And because of frequent extended hours spent at school, she also provided her mother's home phone, where she sometimes stayed overnight because of her long commute.

Ms. Christine would arrive at school before the sun rose. Every morning on my way to work, I would drop Alex off at the before-school day care (called Adventure Club) that was housed within the elementary school building's lunchroom. On one particularly difficult morning (and there were many) Alex had a major meltdown because of one innocent comment. The evening before, we had taken him for a haircut and afterwards he overheard his father say that he thought the stylist had not done a very good job. We were unaware that Alex overheard the comment and was now sensitive to the way his hair looked.

The following morning when we entered the Adventure Club room, one of the staff said, "Alex, your hair!" Immediately Alex thought that she was making fun of him because of the misperceived statement the night before. Of course, the staff member was not teasing him, but because she did not specifically say that his hair looked nice, he automatically assumed the worst. He ran out of the room very upset. I hurried after him trying to explain the misunderstanding, but naturally mother's kind words have no worth when a meltdown is in the works. He emotionally escalated as I tried to coax him back into the lunchroom. Now splayed on the hallway floor screaming and crying, I desperately and unsuccessfully tried to calm him down. He most likely sensed my anxiety, as I knew that I would be late for work if I did not leave soon. The clock was ticking.

His screams were obviously heard throughout the school building because suddenly Ms. Christine appeared from the complete opposite end of the building. She briskly started walking down the long hallway toward us and I swear that a bright, white light illuminated her, like an apparition of the Virgin Mary! When she reached us, she simply got down on her knees and started to work her magic, asking Alex what was wrong. She told him that they could go to her room and talk about it, eventually distracting him from his angst. The tightness in my chest released as I watched the two of them calmly walk down the hall to her classroom, allowing me to head for the door. It takes an exceptional individual to handle children with special needs and Ms. Christine possessed skill and commitment beyond comparison. Whatever she was getting paid, in my mind it was not enough.

In one of my many conversations with Ms. Christine, we discussed Alex's sensory issues with sight, sound, touch, and smell. He was very sensitive to smell and would become upset if the aroma was offensive to him. It was important to explain new odors in the classroom that dealt with projects, such as strong glue or overwhelming magic marker fumes. Alex would have to be moved if the smell was too close to him. He would frequently sniff other children as well as the teacher and her assistants that worked in the self-contained classroom. Ms. Christine taught him to comment on the smell instead of sniffing at others. Picture the height of a teacher against the height of a five-year-old. Thankfully, the butt-sniffing was squashed early on.

Ms. Christine went above and beyond to assist the staff in Adventure Club during Alex's elementary years. Adventure Club was not part of her responsibility, but there she was graciously offering her expertise. Knowing that autistic children process more effectively using visuals, she assembled a story board to track movement in Alex's morning routine. Each activity listed on the board was displayed chronologically and was identified with a picture. The board guided him to hang his coat and backpack in a designated area, eat his breakfast, place his trash in the receptacle, and take part in a chosen activity. As Alex accomplished each task listed, he would place a Velcro circle next to the picture, deeming the activity completed. This allowed Alex to understand daily expectations, have some sense of control, and provide a smooth transition from one activity to the next.

The last picture on the story board showed Alex transitioning from Adventure Club to the regular school setting. This prompted awareness to Alex that his school day was about to begin. Not all days went smoothly. One problematic morning an Adventure Club staff member was squatting down facing the story board, attempting to get Alex to acknowledge the start of his school day. He was not cooperating, eventually went into sensory overload and with the strength of a six-year-old kicked her in the lower back. I thought for sure that Alex would be expelled from Adventure Club.

The traumatized staff member was out on sick leave for a few days as she recovered. When she returned to work, I profusely apologized for Alex's unacceptable behavior. I was stunned when she displayed no hard feelings, seemingly taking the assault in stride. As we continued to discuss the incident, I learned that this sweet lady was currently attending a university to become an elementary school teacher. As it turned out, the Adventure Club staff member, Ms. Tammy, would become Alex's fourth and fifth grade teacher. She obviously had a heart of gold to suffer an injury, then return to work with a casual forgiveness. That is true dedication that deserves complete admiration. I honestly could not put myself in the "heart of a teacher" category.

Social Stories are an effective tool for teaching learning disabled children. The stories offer easy to read text, alongside relevant pictures that describe a situation or concept in terms of social cues and provide appropriate common responses in a format that is easy for a child to understand. Ms. Christine effectively used social stories to address Alex's lack of anger control and encourage acceptable behavior.

One of many cleverly administered stories was, "Use the Turtle Trick to Keep from Losing Your Temper." It continued:

- Pretend you are a turtle
- Go inside your shell
- Calm down and think
- Talk, don't hit
- Don't be mean
- When you are feeling angry or upset
- Go inside your shell
- Take some deep breaths and relax
- Think of a good plan to solve the problem

The last page adorably displayed a proud cartoon turtle with a trophy and the written words, "Trying Turtle Award."

Additionally, to reinforce good behavior in the classroom Ms. Christine incorporated a token system that allowed Alex to earn credit for rewards. When he accumulated enough tokens, he excitedly chose from the many prizes in the elaborate treasure box, from stickers, to gummy bears, to plastic bugs and dinosaurs, to hot wheels, to vouchers for computer time. Ms. Christine also lovingly doled out plenty of positive praise as reinforcement, always noting how proud she was of him.

A Daily Behavior Sheet was developed by Ms. Christine that addressed Alex's specific needs and goals. When he did not comply with requests at school, the daily report was marked accordingly, always including extra hand-written notes to promote clarity. This tool was instrumental in allowing Mike and me to address behavior related problems with Alex once at home, where the distraction of the school setting was eliminated. Collaboration between teacher and parents allowed for discipline reinforcements applied at school, to be consistent with discipline at home.

As no surprise, that year Ms. Christine won the famed "Crystal Apple Award," an honor presented to public school educators who have made a positive impact on the lives of their students. And that very same year, Ms. Christine was deservedly awarded the prestigious "Christa McAuliffe, Pioneer in Education Award" given to an outstanding educator who exhibits innovation, motivation, and remarkable spirit. We were so very fortunate that Ms. Christine was in our lives!

The day that Alex turned six, our second son Austin was four days away from joining our family. This pregnancy would culminate with a planned cesarean. I had no desire to go through the painful and unsuccessful experience as with the first attempt at delivery. With Alex's unpredictable behaviors, we were not sure how he would react to a new baby receiving all the attention, so we thoughtfully considered how we would introduce Alex to his new little brother. After obtaining several suggestions, we asked Alex to write on a small, colorful piece of construction paper, "Hi Austin, I'm your big brother Alex." Then Alex glued a picture of himself to the note. At the hospital, Alex placed the note inside the bassinet, so (in theory) his baby brother could see the note. With the customary practice of receiving newborn baby gifts, we did not want to risk that Alex would feel left out and possibly cause a disruption, so we purchased a few Hot Wheels and some candy, placed them in a small gift bag and presented the loot to him in the hospital room. Alex felt proud to be a big brother and happily received new toys. All was good in his world. Amazingly, his behavior was perfect.

*Welcoming his little brother in the hospital.*

Up until the birth of my second son, Alex had not displayed any detectable affection towards me, that I can recall. But an unexpected exchange took place between me and my six-year-old that completely caught me off guard. I was in my recovery room after the cesarean surgery, hooked up to an IV. Various strange medical devices dotted the room. The pain-relieving drugs were kicking in and with no makeup I looked ragged at best. Gaining sixty-five pounds and working full time during the last month of pregnancy had really wiped me out. I had not thought twice about my appearance or considered what that image would communicate to Alex. When he first entered my room, he looked devastated and ran over to my bedside whimpering. He was frightened and tried to crawl onto the bed. I gave him a big hug and immediately assured him that I was just fine, and he did not need to worry. In the most upbeat tone that I could muster, I explained the purpose of the wires and tubes, and then I could see the anxiety melt away from his face. At age six, it was the first time that I had felt a true emotionally heartfelt response from Alex.

Sensory issues would continue. Every weekday morning, after I dropped Alex at Adventure Club, he would immediately remove his shoes once inside the classroom. Attempting to get them back on his feet would cause the staff extra effort and stress when it was time to transition either to an outdoor activity or to his regular school day. After several conversations with Alex's support team, we suspected tactile sensory issues with his feet. Being unable to handle shoes was never noted in preschool, but then I remembered a note from his Lighthouse preschool days stating that he did not like walking in shaving cream with his bare feet, one of the many sensory activities offered. The slimy, squishy feeling between his toes overloaded his senses.

As the team considered a solution for my shoeless child, we agreed on the possibility that his discomfort may not be the shoes per se causing the torment. The irritation may be the bulky toe seam in his socks that aggravated his toes when shoes were worn. After days of research and phone calls, I discovered a company that manufactured children's "seamless toe" socks. I ordered several pairs through the mail, anxiously waiting up to three weeks for them to ship. In today's environment of immediate gratification, lengthy shipping with no option to expedite would never be tolerated, but this was the late nineties. Eager to try on the new socks, we immediately tore open the package when it arrived and slipped the soft, cushy coverings on Alex's feet. Then came the moment of truth. The shoes were placed on his feet. Glorious success! He was happy with how the socks felt and was able to keep his shoes on all day.

Eventually the seamless socks grew in popularity as recognition of sensory issues grew, and I was able to find them at a local shoe store. Of course, the special socks were three times as expensive as regular socks, but worth every penny. After about seven years of purchasing seamless socks, Alex finally outgrew the need.

Causing additional sensory aggravation for Alex were those pesky clothing tags. He balked at the hard, scratchy feeling of the tag rubbing against his delicate skin. I certainly could understand that agony and I went about cutting every tag out of his clothing.

Writing for Alex was a struggle that followed him all the way through college. In early elementary school his writing clearly demonstrated a great need for improvement. The following image shows his journal entry explaining that the Titanic was hit by an iceberg. I can't imagine the time it took for his teacher to decipher, correct, and grade his work.

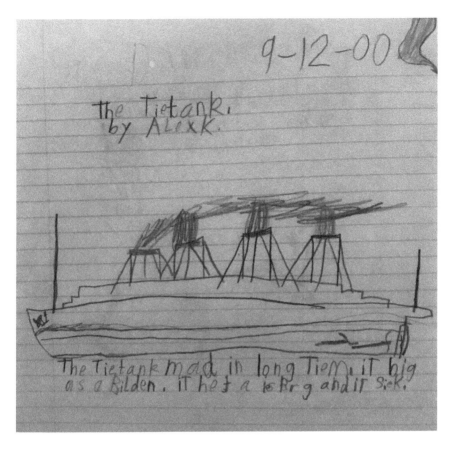

***Translation:*** *The Titanic was made a long time ago. It was as big as a building. It hit an iceberg and it sank.*

On the flip side, Alex's written skills were greatly improved when it came to subjects that he was interested in, such as bugs and dinosaurs. He practically knew them all. Between my mother and mother-in-law, they bestowed many children's books on insects and carnivores. The following image was journaled on the very next page after the Titanic entry. The contrast in spelling and clarity between the two show his capabilities when the subject was appealing, and he had already gained exposure to the content.

The Velociraptor

Velociraptor was a speedy little meat eater. It attacked planteater that were up to five times larger than itself. If i had a Velociraptor i show to avig buiDe.

In his later years, when Alex finally outgrew the juvenile books and the little plastic dinosaurs, beetles, dragonflies, and ladybugs, I held a garage sale. An older woman stopped by and excitedly said, "Oh, my grandson is obsessed with dinosaurs!"

I said, "Have I got a deal for you!"

She happily accepted every prehistoric creature related book and toy for a minimal fee, and I was extremely pleased that another little boy would benefit from the motherload of ancient beast paraphernalia.

Most times Alex's writing reflected the way he spoke. He would inappropriately transpose pronouns such as "he" for "she." He also mispronounced past tense verbs. When he claimed, "I baked a cake," he would pronounce the word "bake-did." For years he'd say, "next by" instead of "next to." "It's next by that door." Or instead of properly saying, "On this day" he would say, "At this day." I was in constant correction mode. However, instead of me repeating a word or phrase correctly, I would say, "Say that again?" or "How does that go?" or "It's next…what?" Always trying to enforce self-correction.

By second grade, ongoing tests concluded that at age eight Alex's language fundamentals were equivalent to a six-year-old. Because of that deficit, Alex was only included part-time in a regular classroom setting for the subjects that caused him the least amount of stress. The partial inclusion strategy tested his abilities to tolerate sounds that could potentially send him into sensory overload. Some common causes were noisy children and their chaotic behaviors, the relentless buzzing of a fluorescent light, and the ear-piercing effect of squeaky chalk on a blackboard.

Hearing sensitivity was prevalent inside as well as outside of the school environment. Our family loved the outdoors and would take frequent hikes in the woods. We occasionally visited one heavily wooded trail that had a large horsefly presence. Alex would get so upset, swatting, and growling as the amplified buzz of those flying nuisances dove past his head. The pests made him so miserable that we finally had to stop visiting that specific park.

Most school days went well. However, one day Alex became highly frustrated with another classmate and severely scratched his face, drawing blood. Fortunately, the parents of the injured child did not press charges, as they certainly had the right. The details leading up to the incident were not shared with me, which lead me to wonder if the event had been provoked. Nevertheless, I was merely asked to ensure that Alex's nails were always kept short, and you can bet that they were. Whew, dodged that bullet!

The postage stamp distribution facility in Kansas City where I was currently working for the Postal Service was the only operation of its kind in the United States. This division was not governed by the local postal district but managed directly by Headquarters in Washington, D.C. So, there was more leeway by management for social events. Our facility Director offered employees the opportunity to take part in "take your child to work day." Back then, the stamp distribution operation used hand-to-hand procedures with very little machinery. At regular mail processing facilities there was always heavy rolling containers of mail, floor trucks bustling about, and sorting machinery with lots of moving parts. Bringing your kid to work at a typical postal processing facility was unheard of. Postal operations would be far too dangerous for youngsters that are notorious for a short attention span and not inclined to consistently be aware of their surroundings.

Because I encouraged every learning opportunity for Alex, I was thrilled that he would have a chance to see where I worked. I signed him up and notified school that he would be out for the day. That morning as we drove into the dark underground cave complex where my office was located, a wide-eyed Alex took in the dusty, jagged, limestone walls, the white-washed, rocky pillars, and encroaching ceiling.

Once inside my office building, he very attentively sat at my cubicle. Part of my day was spent on the phone in Customer Service answering, "Where is my order?" calls. Quite boring for an eight-year-old. But Alex sat patiently (looking at his reptile books) and listened to my conversations, while glancing at my monitor as I flipped from screen to screen to understand the customer's order status.

During our special day, the facility director invited about 25 of us to gather in the conference room with our kids. We all crammed into the small room as he explained how the facility operated. One of the adults in attendance who was sitting next to Alex started talking to him, asking him questions while the director was addressing the room. I was surprised that the adult was showing no respect for the head of the facility and caused Alex to be a distraction. I motioned to get Alex's attention and asked him to be quiet and listen. The adult, without any concern for being disruptive casually said, "Oh, it's my fault, I'm talking to him." I thought to myself, I know! And please don't encourage bad behavior when I'm trying so hard to teach him how to be socially appropriate! I realize that the adult meant well by trying to make him feel included, but they were modeling the wrong social etiquette.

As the day continued, one of my coworkers said that they were surprised that I brought my child to work, implying (my assumption) that a disabled child may have been unable to tolerate the environment. But Alex did great, and I was proud of how he handled the entire eight-and-a-half-hour workday. The next day at school my eight-year-old wrote in his journal, *"I went to my mom's work. She worked mail and computer. She worked hard, then harder, then she stopped."* That made me smile.

*A good day at the office.*

Alex was extraordinary at catching all kinds of insects and reptiles. He had a handheld bug container with a viewing screen that always housed some sort of critter. He caught grasshoppers by the dozen and would gently feed each of them a blade of grass. By now, there was nothing wrong with those fine motor skills, although he still could not tie his shoes. However, that was my fault and I unapologetically blame Velcro shoes. Safety first. In due time, conquering shoelaces would come.

*Feeding a hungry grasshopper.*

One sunny, cool afternoon in early Spring, Alex came upon a snake that was sunning itself on a rock in the local park. Naturally, he caught the slow-moving, cold-blooded reptile and proudly presented it to Mike and me, pleading to bring the slinky serpent home. After wearing us down, we relented and set up a glass aquarium with a warming light and terrain resembling a grassy meadow. After about a year or so of having to trek to the pet store for meals of crickets and live, hairless baby mice, we talked Alex into releasing the snake back into the wild; for its own good, of course. We returned to the same location in the park where the snake was found and set it free without incident. I certainly was not sad to see it slither away into the tall weeds, hopefully reunited with its family.

Like most young children, Alex was very curious. He liked bugs and was easily distracted by them. Like a dog following a scent, if my budding entomologist saw a butterfly, off he'd go without any regard for boundaries or safety. And although I kept a close eye on him when we were away from the protection of home, I gave him the freedom to explore, carefully watching him from a distance. I did not want to stifle his curiosity or make him afraid to investigate his world.

However, the freedom to explore was most likely not appreciated by his teachers when one day he escaped the school building undetected and could not be located. After a frantic twenty-minute search, a teacher found him unharmed on the far side of a field, across the street from the school. My guess is he was most likely hunting for insects. I received a phone call informing me that he was missing only after they had found him. The rattled tone in the teacher's voice left no doubt that she had been petrified.

As a result of that frightening episode, Alex was assigned a peer buddy to ensure that he transitioned from class to class without wandering. Alex preferred to change classrooms without a tail and worked on improving his attention to task. The peer buddy was eventually excused from duty, but Alex still needed to be in view of a teacher to prevent him from entering other rooms. As time passed, he was allowed to transition from class to class independently, but a responsible adult was still designated to ensure that my wanderlust child appropriately arrived at his destination.

Visual Arts class was one of the subjects where Alex had no adverse behaviors, according to his report cards. So, when I read that the school district was offering a summer drawing class for children ages eight to ten, I asked Alex if he wanted to attend. He agreed without hesitation. Because Alex still had social and behavioral concerns, I was a little apprehensive about leaving behind my nine-year-old son in a totally new environment, where he would need to focus for three hours with no meltdowns.

The drawing classes were being held on Saturdays at a nearby high school that typically housed over fifteen hundred students, and the art teacher was a man from a neighboring town. The massive school building and summer art teacher were new and unfamiliar to Alex. To ease his anxiety of the unknown, Mike and I took Alex to the high school a few days before classes were to begin, locating his classroom, the bathrooms, and visual landmarks to help him navigate. When the first Saturday of summer art classes arrived, we drove to the enormous brick building and ambled inside to meet the new teacher. I discreetly informed the young man that Alex was autistic and that he may present some unusual behaviors or make growling noises as he frequently did when frustration set in. I gave the instructor my phone number and said he should call if he ran into any uncontrollable matters. I genuinely expected to receive an early call with a request to retrieve my child. To my surprise, no phone call came.

After three hours passed, I drove back to the school and tentatively entered the classroom. Alex was in a great mood and proudly showed me his drawings. The class was learning to sketch comic and Disney characters. Since my drawing skills stop at stick figures, I was certainly impressed with Alex's ability to draw Mickey Mouse and still life objects. I asked the teacher if he had had any issues and he said, "I had no problems with Alex. I wouldn't have even known he was autistic if you hadn't told me." That was my first realization that we should continue to develop Alex's artistic talent. An art therapist once told me that art is a natural way for a child to express himself, to work through problems, to explore ideas safely, to build self-confidence and to learn how to enjoy creating. This was certainly true for Alex.

At the end of each school year, Alex was enrolled in six weeks of academic summer school. The consistency to retain learned behaviors was crucial during his elementary years. He seemed less stressed during the summer which allowed his personality and unique interpretations of life to shine. One summer at age seven a note came home from the teacher that offered insight into Alex's sense of humor.

Miss Vanessa wrote:

*"Alex is doing such a wonderful job this summer. I see him constantly trying new things and enjoying new challenges. He is truly a joy to be around with his playfulness and funny sayings. The other day a staff member was tapping his pen on a clipboard and Alex turned around, looked at him and said, "Who's pecking?" We all thought it was hilarious. Thanks for letting us spend time with such a great kid."*

Working full time and spending a great deal of "at home" time enforcing homework and tending to daily household tasks, I sometimes failed to experience Alex's humor. Letters from teachers that shared inspiring stories and kind words meant the world to me and offered me the privilege of seeing Alex from other's perspectives.

Although Alex was making great progress, difficult behaviors continued during the regular school year when he was pressured to comply with challenging activities that triggered sensory overload. Most days his daily behavior sheet showed that he was doing well, but occasionally I would read teacher notes that said, "Today Alex slapped someone on the neck and ripped their magazine" or "Alex became angry and refused to work on a group project." To combat this behavior and allow Alex to learn how to self-regulate before escalating, the principal offered to forfeit a small, dark closet located in the quiet, front offices. The closet was converted into a calming, safe space where Alex could pull himself together before he spiraled into a full meltdown. I was grateful for the principal's generosity and bought some sensory toys for the closet. When Alex felt himself starting to emotionally escalate in the classroom, he would ask to go to the safe space, where his senses were calmed by the elimination of bright lights, loud sounds, and any unusual smells from a classroom project. Once his emotions calmed, he would return to class. There was a fine line between needing to calm down and simply not wanting to work. Ms. Tammy, his fourth and fifth grade teacher, masterfully managed that fine line.

Ms. Tammy was reliably passionate when it came to her students. She demanded that Alex do his very best at all times. We exchanged several hand-written notes and had many phone conversations related to her frustrations when Alex was less than motivated and not completely accountable, when she knew he was capable. Unfortunately, those characteristics were present at home too when he was pressured to complete assignments. As much as I would have preferred a stress-free evening after a long, tiring day at work, I had no magic wand to change Alex's unmotivated and unfocused behaviors. I had become pretty savvy with bribing for results, but when Alex was ready to shut down, no amount of candy, computer time, cartoons, or toys could turn things around. We would start working on lessons right after dinner. There were many nights when it took all evening to complete the assignments. Alex required breaks after small segments of focus. We would work for a while, then break with a snack, or a favorite toy, or TV time. Completion of homework was time-consuming, and I struggled to keep that pace each and every night. In addition, I had a four-year-old that deserved attention too. Balancing Alex's needs with my desire to cuddle on the couch with Austin and his favorite book, watch a Disney video together, or play with toys and exchange dialogue, was a constant pull on my psyche.

It remained that Alex had trouble completing the amount of schoolwork doled out in fifth grade, and I was at the end of my rope with no more effort to give. I made a call to Ms. Karen, a special needs resource teacher at the elementary school. I explained that the level of coursework was more than what we could tackle in the evenings. I did not want to reduce Alex's work commitments, as he was already academically behind, plus I wanted him to be ready to advance to sixth grade. So, Ms. Karen offered to work with Alex in the mornings before school to complete the assignments that we could not quite finish the evening before. Her help was most appreciated, restoring some respite and sanity to our evenings.

Not all school challenges were generated by Alex. During fifth grade, his regular education teacher Ms. Tammy, had informed me that Alex had reverted to hitting others when frustrated. The elimination of physical aggression was a behavior goal in his Individual Education Plan that according to teacher reports was mastered the previous year. We had agreed to keep the "no hitting" goal in his IEP to identify any regression.

Federal guidelines require that school personnel report on IEP objectives on a quarterly basis, identifying each goal as either "Mastered", "Making Progress", "No Progress", or "Not Initiated." I was perplexed that Alex was once again hitting others and asked Ms. Tammy what the special education teacher (assigned as Alex's case manager) was doing to avert this behavior. Turns out, the special education teacher rarely visited the regular education classroom where she was assigned to carry out her teaching and oversight duties. It was then that I realized that I had not received the last two federally mandated quarterly IEP progress reports from the special education teacher. When I asked Ms. Tammy about the reports, she stated that she had not received copies of the progress reports either.

I immediately requested an emergency IEP meeting with school personnel that made up Alex's support team. During the IEP meeting I asked the special education teacher about the missing reports, and she blatantly lied to my face. She claimed that she had given me, as well as Ms. Tammy the completed quarterly progress reports and then with an "I'm-smarter-than-you" smirk, she proceeded to cavalierly drop them on the table in front of us. I scooped up the report and immediately flipped the pages to the "no-hitting" goal and was irritated to read that she had marked it Mastered - 100% achieved. Had she been in the classroom doing her assigned job, she would have known that the hitting goal needed to be revisited. At this point my blood was boiling, but I did not call her out in front of the entire IEP team.

Directly after the meeting, I wrote a strongly worded, but professional letter to the principal (who had attended the meeting), highlighting the special education teacher's lies and requested that she be replaced with someone else to serve as Alex's case manager. To emphasize the importance and sincerity of my request, I courtesy copied the school district's Director of Pupil Services. The following day, I received a call from the principal stating that the inept teacher was reassigned to a completely different elementary school within the district, placing her in a self-contained room (limiting her mobility), where she would be monitored by superiors. I was quite surprised, as I had not expected her consequences to be that harsh and surmised that there must have been some other underlying controversy. Honestly, I would have looked the other way regarding the missing quarterly reports, but being lied to and treated like a fool was intolerable. Challenges with disabled kiddos are hard enough to manage, no one needs a misguided teacher making it harder.

Throughout elementary school the Autism Project funded two different therapists that visited Alex in our home weekly after school. His occupational therapist, Miss Jessi worked on social awareness skills. His speech therapist, Miss Robin focused on improving academics such as the use of correct verb tenses and pronouns, as well as the understanding of idioms and sarcasm. Alex's thinking was very literal, and he could not interpret phrases like "it's raining cats and dogs," "you're pulling my leg" or "hold your horses," until he was purposely taught their meaning. There were over thirty idioms on the list that were translated for Alex.

If you search the internet for idiomatic expressions, the results show that there are at least 25,000 in the English language. Understandably, it was impossible to teach every expression, as I soon learned. Part of my weekend was spent catching up on household chores. One Saturday, Alex and I were in the laundry room, where my sewing machine was located. I was preparing to catch up on a stack of ripped underarm t-shirts, split pants seams, missing buttons, and unraveled bath towel hems that were starting to fray. I reached for the cord to plug in the machine and Alex said, "I want to plug it in." I said, "Okay, but be careful." He slowly lined up the plug and pushed it into the socket. Immediately he jerked his hand back with a slight yelp. I said, "Ooooh, it bit you, didn't it?" I continued, "You have to remember to keep your fingers off the prongs when you're pushing in the plug." He didn't verbalize any response, but I could see his little wheels turning.

About a year later, I heard Alex telling his younger cousin, who was visiting our home and was getting ready to plug in a gaming device, "Watch out, there's a bug inside there and it can bite you!" I winced as I realized I had unintentionally misled him all that time but had to laugh. With a chuckle I explained to both boys that there were no biting bugs in the wall, that what Alex felt a year ago was an electric shock. Idioms and abstract phrasing spewed out of my mouth so easily in everyday language that I never thought twice about my words. That episode taught me how easily misperception happened for Alex.

When Alex was nine years old his Speech Therapist Miss Robin attempted to explain to him that he was Autistic. She used a comprehensive, published storybook that covered a host of autistic characteristics. By now, Alex was pretty high-functioning. His verbal skills were improving. He never had self-stimulating behaviors such as hand flapping, spinning, or rocking. When Miss Robin presented those self-stimulating characteristics as part of autistic behavior, Alex became very agitated, boisterously vocalizing his disdain. He refused to continue, requiring the session to end early. He was alarmed and confused to be categorized with that level of severe behavior. He was in a funk for at least a month after that session and Miss Robin never again approached the subject. In hindsight, Miss Robin should have only used Alex's distinct characteristics to explain his learning and behavioral challenges.

Alex's occupational therapist, Miss Jessi focused on improving behaviors such as awareness and control over his emotions, the ability to read subtle body language and facial expressions (boredom, confusion, disappointment, etc.), and to communicate with words rather than physical aggression, growling or roaring like a dinosaur when upset.

One day while shopping at a department store, Alex became distressed when I would not purchase a Lego set. They were expensive even back then and he already had a mountain of them. He was relentless and could not redirect his thoughts from the desired item. I held my ground and when we arrived home, I meticulously explained why he could not have everything he wanted. During my lecture, he was sitting at the dining room table, with his elbow propped on the table, hand holding up his head, shoulders slumped, and wearing a blank stare on his face. When I finally stopped talking, he droned, "Mom, can you tell what I'm thinking?" I said, "What?" He said, "I'm bored." I smiled to myself and thought, "Well he's certainly catching on to facial expressions and sarcasm."

One of the behaviors Miss Jessi focused on was Alex's penchant for interrupting adults when they were speaking. I'm sure there were many instances at school, but personally Alex would loudly talk over a conversation in play when I was on the phone or speaking in person with another adult. He had difficulty waiting for attention. Miss Jessi crafted a personalized social story with corresponding pictures to help Alex gain a more accurate understanding of social situations and expected behaviors. Here's how the story progressed:

- If adults visit my house
- If someone's on the phone
- At school, if teachers are talking
- When I want to talk to an adult, they may be busy
- And I might have to wait, which makes me mad
- So, I'll say "excuse me"
- And wait
- If I wait a little bit
- I could sit
- Or stand
- If I wait a long time
- I may draw
- Or play
- This way I won't get mad

- And we'll ALL be ready to talk
- The End

Alex quickly learned to say, "excuse me." The "waiting" part took a while to successfully master.

At home Mike and I continued to teach appropriate social behaviors. One Saturday morning, me, Mike, Alex, and little brother Austin drove to IHOP for a late breakfast. We pulled up to the curb where the sidewalk led directly to the front doors of the restaurant. Alex immediately jumped out of the car and swiftly walked towards the entry doors. Mike and I both said, "Hey, wait for the rest of your family." Mike was busy unbuckling Austin from his car seat, and I was in the back seat on the far side of the car grabbing the diaper bag. A man and woman with two small children were walking into the restaurant and Alex followed them in, as if he were a part of their family. I'm sure they were a little surprised when the waitress said, "Table for five?" Mike and I eventually caught up with Alex, apologized to the family and then explained to Alex why he needed to wait and walk in with his own family.

Alex was stretched to his limit academically, so we never promoted extracurricular activities during the school week. We naively thought that he could not handle more than what was already on his plate. To our amazement, at the beginning of fifth grade Alex informed Mike and me that he wanted to play the violin. He had not previously shown any commitment to elective courses, so we were a little hesitant. We said, "Let us think about it." That night we contemplated the expense of buying a violin, but still hadn't come to a final decision. The very next day Alex came home with a one-page form for us to complete that allowed him to rent a violin from the school district for a measly twenty dollars for the year. We said, "Well, let's sign you up!"

Alex continued to play violin through his senior year of high school. As a parent, experiencing eight years of musical progression, from the assaulting cringe-worthy notes at the fifth-grade concerts to the harmonious orchestra performances of twelfth grade was enormously fulfilling. Private violin lessons started during middle school when we pleasantly realized that Alex was going to remain committed to the instrument.

With Mike and I both working full time, we were always on the go. The kids were our focus, which left very little time for ourselves. To maintain a sense of balance, we each took a separate evening off during the week for a much-needed respite and adult conversation. Mike spent his free evening playing softball with the guys and I played volleyball with my mom and two of my sisters. The exercise and adult interaction rejuvenated our minds.

As most parents do, we spent many evenings looking over school reports, helping with homework assignments, tackling mountains of laundry, ensuring showers were taken, and selecting our books for bedtime reading. I cooked most weekends, however dinners during the week were spent at a "sit down and be served" restaurant.

We were fortunate to be able to factor the cost of eating out into our budget. At times we lived from paycheck to paycheck and had to tighten our belts when it came to entertainment like concerts, movies, and vacations, but we were blessed to be able to afford a decent meal out. Don't get me wrong, occasionally McDonalds, Burger King, Sonic, or Wendy's made it into the meal rotation, but it wasn't very often. Drive-thru was typically the result of having to be at an afterschool event, such as an orchestra concert or parent/teacher conferences.

Relaxingly sitting together with our boys at dinner allowed us to collectively unwind and connect after making it through our busy days of work and school. Each family member advantageously ordered what they were in the mood to eat, preventing waste and I was beyond thrilled that I escaped meal preparation, cooking, and cleaning!

# Chapter 5. Middle School

Leaving elementary school behind, we started to focus on the big transition to Junior High. Of course, this meant that Alex would require an advance walk-through of the new school building to become acclimated. We arranged a time with his new school case manager, and a week before school was in session we walked to each classroom in chronological order, as listed on his daily class schedule. We additionally scoped out the special needs resource room, as well as the restrooms, cafeteria, and gymnasiums. This would be the first year that Alex utilized a locker, so we located his assigned storage space and practiced opening and closing with his unique number combination. This would also be the first year that he consistently changed classrooms for all subjects. To aid in this transition the resource teacher developed a small, hand-held picture schedule to offer discreetness and ensure that he arrived at the correct location. All these measures were necessary preparation to help reduce Alex's anxiety until his routine became familiar.

With the new IEP drafted and approved we were moving on up. A lot of the same behaviors and academic deficiencies still plagued Alex, so the educational focus remained similar, but just at a higher grade level. Unacceptable behaviors and coping skills were improving so instead of being in the special needs resource classroom setting between 21% and 60% of his school day, the new goal was to decrease time spent there to less than 21% of his school day.

The academic portion of the IEP document required Alex to:

- Increase math skills.

    - Adding, subtracting, two-step story problems, multiplication facts through 12, and divide whole numbers.

- Advance spelling levels.

  – Gain the ability to identify misspelled sight words in writing assignments.

- Improve verbal and written communication.

  – Practice speaking and writing activities using correct pronouns, verb tenses, and correct plural forms.

To establish Alex's accountability for compliance, he was primed each morning for academic and behavioral expectations within his natural setting of the classroom. The regular education teacher was his primary coach regarding demonstration of appropriate school behaviors. He was also coached by other staff members to encourage generalization of responding to directions from all adults. Again, social stories were used to help Alex process his anger and improve self-control when he became frustrated with peers and adults. To remain consistent with successful past practices, he was also provided a cool down spot, that was equipped with favored sensory and science items to encourage calming. Behavioral interventions documented in the education plan stated that Alex would:

- Demonstrate self-control using a respectful voice when angry versus harming others. No growling, lying or hurtful words.

- Improve skills and school related behaviors needed to contribute to and remain with a group while working on academics.

- Focus on the teacher. Stay in own space allowing other students to view what teacher wants to show the group.

- Use a cool down pass to the drinking fountain to give an opportunity to regain control of emotions and behavior.

- Remove himself to a designated safe area in the classroom until calm, when feeling threatened or wanting to hurt someone. Use a stress ball or science manipulatives for five to ten minutes.

If cannot calm in this short time, go to the cool down area in the school office. May read, use sensory items, or lie down. Use social stories for processing the problem.

- Practice processing with a familiar adult and unfamiliar adult to help him generalize this ability to all adults in charge at school.

- Work with the adults in charge to make restitution when he has had a problem.

Bullying typically becomes more prominent at the middle school level, as was apparent when Alex integrated into junior high (6th through 8th grades).

Oddities in behavior and speech made him an easy target for harassment by other students. One afternoon while changing classrooms, a smug boy who obviously felt superior to my fledgling sixth grader stood in front of Alex's locker and would not allow him access.

Alex needed to drop off his books from the previous class, grab his books for the next subject and get to class before the bell rang. For those who have attended a large middle school (700+ students) you may be familiar with hallway crowding and the short timeframe that is allowed in between classes. Alex asked the taunting boy to step aside, and the boy refused. With time ticking away Alex began to emotionally escalate. With his anxiety rising by the second, and the tormenting boy still maintaining his ground, Alex reared back and punched him in the face. As a result, Alex was awarded with an in-school suspension for three days.

The repercussions provided me with an opportunity to teach Alex that he could not be the first to hit someone, however, I countered that if someone had hit him first, he was well within his rights to defend himself. Later that week, I was explaining the locker episode to my childless hairdresser, and he was appalled at the unfairness of Alex's punishment. I expressed that it may have been somewhat unfair to

Alex, however it was advantageous to teach the lesson now, as once he turned 18, he would be legally responsible for his actions.

Teaching the subtleties of social awareness and decorum was a constant task. One pleasant afternoon Alex and I had been shopping in a nearby town. On our way home I was cruising down a side street that had a posted speed limit of thirty-five miles per hour. Apparently, I was exceeding the speed limit and the next thing I knew, there were party lights in the rearview mirror. I pulled over and cordially addressed the police officer as he strolled up to my window. He said, "Did you know you were speeding?" I said, "No, I hadn't realized." He said, "I passed you coming from the opposite direction, noticed you were speeding and flashed my headlights." Whether he did or not, I never noticed. The officer said, "Since you did not heed my warning, I decided to turn around and pull you over."

I explained that we were running errands and we were now on our way home. The conversation was polite, but the officer had an air of superiority with an authoritarian father-like tone, bordering on condescension. After about ten minutes of discussion, he decided to only give me a warning and ended with saying, "You need to pay attention and slow down." As the officer walked away Alex chirped from the front passenger seat, "I'll help with that." The officer did not hear exactly what Alex said, but he was clearly agitated with a tone that left no doubt that he was not taking any guff from this little kid. The officer trudged back to my window and irritatingly barked to Alex, "What did you say?" Visions of the Cops television show came to mind, and I feared that I would be yanked from the car and cuffed. I had already done enough explaining by then, so I merely sat back and let Alex speak for himself. Alex spoke to the officer using his improper grammatical speech, implying that he would watch my speed and help keep me in compliance. After listening to Alex's immature and incorrect dialect, I believe that the officer was wise enough to conclude that Alex was not some Smart Aleck kid, and that he was sincere with his remarks. Luckily, the officer calmed his gruff attitude, and we were released. I immediately explained to Alex that in the future if I was stopped by law enforcement, he should remain quiet because his words could be mistaken for sarcasm. Poor kiddo. He was just trying to be helpful.

During middle school Alex's self-awareness grew concerning his inability to establish and maintain friendships. That awareness was aided by his classmates who were also now beginning to recognize and understand their peer's behavioral eccentricities and form their own opinions. Alex's sadness of this new realization was interfering with his academics, and he appeared to show signs of depression. With a growing concern, I requested an IEP meeting with Alex's educational support team and explained my worries about his dropping grades and increasing unhappiness. Thankfully, the educators approved an IEP modification that allowed Alex to participate in the Extended Day Program for additional help and study time, as well as provided him with a weekly thirty-minute counseling session. As weeks passed, these modifications seemed to be helping.

To promote social engagement among students, the school hosted an occasional Friday Fun Night with loud music, dancing, and snacks. The chatter, volume and energy at these events was exhilarating. The teen boys could be found in one of the gyms playing basketball or watching the girls dance to the DJ's thumping tunes or scarfing down greasy pizza, candy bars, and sugary drinks that were offered in the main lobby.

The giggly, chatty tween girls flitted between the two gymnasiums, the food area, and the photography booth, where they collectively glossed their lips and made kissy faces for their cherished memento. As a PTA member, I volunteered to chaperone these events in hopes that Alex would feel comfortable attending and possibly make a friend. Alas, the high-energy sensory stimulation was just too much for him to handle. He became overwhelmed and stepped outside of the school building in the evening darkness to calm himself. Bless his heart, he was trying his best to fit in.

Immediately after Alex stepped outside, a female parent volunteer came up to me and with an air of superiority and in a snobbish tone said, "We do not allow the children to leave the building at these events." I paused for a moment to collect my thoughts. I intended to say to her, "That's my son, he's in sensory overload and needs to go outside to decompress," but at that moment another word option for decompress crowded my brain, and I meant to finish the sentence with "he needs to go outside to compose himself." But what actually came out of my mouth was, "That's my son, he's in sensory overload and he needs to go outside to *decompose*." Immediately she disgustingly glared at me like I was an idiot, raised up on the balls of her feet, stuck her nose in the air and pivoted away in a huff. I laughed out loud at the farce of that entire exchange, as she scurried away. She obviously could not have cared less about what was really going on. She was only looking for someone to boss around. And then the word for a *female dog* entered my mind.

We lived two blocks away from the middle school so there was no bus service in our neighborhood. I drove Alex to school every morning on my way to work. One chilly, gray morning as we pulled into the school parking lot, I asked Alex if he was going to attend the upcoming Friday Fun Night and he said, "No, I just feel like I'm in everyone's shadow." I was taken aback by his keen perception, and then my heart sank realizing that I was falling short at helping him make friends or feeling like he belonged. It was mistaken guilt, but still my guilt.

Alex started to make troubling comments around age twelve, signaling despair. Choking on his words he would say to me, "I don't have any friends" and "I wish I was dead." I remained strong in front of Alex, but inside my heart was breaking. At this point, I was attending several monthly Autism support groups and inquired with the parents and professionals in attendance for some direction. Within two weeks, Alex was enrolled in one-on-one therapy sessions with a female child psychologist who was familiar with Autism and came highly recommended. Dr. Selina had a very sweet demeanor, a positive outlook and possessed a kind spirit that immediately put me and Alex at ease.

Before each therapy session began, Dr. Selina, me, and Alex would sit in her dimly lit room, on her comfortable, overstuffed couches. I would convey my concerns regarding Alex's disturbing comments and behaviors then I would leave the room, and the two of them would talk by themselves. Dr. Selina helped Alex to dissect and understand his feelings. I was not privy to their discussions, as that remained confidential between the two of them. And I trusted that if there were any crucial elements that needed to be addressed by me, Dr. Selina would have confided in me. For a few years Alex remained eager to attend sessions with Dr. Selina and they seemed to be helping.

As time passed, Dr. Selina realized similarities with some of her other young patients who lacked the ability to emotionally connect. Within her practice, she pioneered a new concept whereas four or five of her struggling children would attend a weekly group session. The weekly session would allow each child to openly discuss their obstacles with the group. The desired goal for the youngsters was to realize that their peers were experiencing the same problems and then not feel so isolated. My hope was that Alex would make a connection and gain a friend. I dropped Alex at the main door of Dr. Selina's building before each session, not entering the office as to retain the anonymity of all the group patients. Alex attended for a few months and said that the sessions were helpful, however, his lack of being able to connect emotionally was still an obstacle and he grew tired of the group sessions.

At one of the previously attended Autism Conferences, I sat through a presentation given by a research scientist who worked in a medical lab. He explained that the gut and the brain had a direct relationship. Certain foods could cause "brain fog." The doctor also believed that antibiotics and acetaminophen somehow removed good bacteria in the gut, causing dysfunction in the brain. As a baby, Alex experienced problems with ear infections. Beginning at age nine months, he was on antibiotics for four months until the infection finally cleared. Two more ear infections lasting about three months each, would cause him grief between the ages of two and three. During those time frames, many nights were spent administering antibiotics and acetaminophen while rocking Alex back to sleep in the early morning hours.

As the scientist continued his lecture, he explained that his laboratory offered urine and blood tests that could identify an individual's food allergies. By removing the identified foods from the diet, Autistic symptoms could be alleviated. And by replacing the good bacteria in the stomach with products like probiotics or enzymes, the brain could function properly. So, I thought, let's give it a try.

After shelling out four hundred dollars for the test, Alex's bloodwork showed a moderate to high reaction to wheat and dairy, suggesting that those ingredients (gluten and casein) should be removed from his diet. Gluten Free/Casein Free (GF/CF) foods were not found in the grocery stores back then, making the suggested diet extremely difficult to administer. There were a few gluten-free flour options starting to emerge online, but they were very expensive and excruciatingly time consuming to prepare a final edible product. The only practical alternative was to eliminate those foods from Alex's diet. By now, Alex was already hooked on bread and cheese, two of his favorite foods and was not willing to give them up. To this day, he's never passed on a slice of pizza.

As an alternative to the GF/CF diet, the conference highlighted an all-fungal enzyme capsule to be taken before each meal. The enzyme was designed to eliminate the adverse effects in the gut and therefore allow the brain to function with greater clarity. Because Alex would be required to take them directly before lunch during school hours, a doctor's note was necessary. I purchased the costly enzymes for fifty dollars, obtained the required documentation from Alex's pediatrician and the test phase began. After about two months Alex confirmed that the enzymes were not helping him, and he stopped taking them. My thoughts ventured back to that very wise teacher who shared the cautionary advice about the many solutions being offered to remove autistic symptoms and the fact that Autism has no cure.

At one of the PTA meetings, I learned that the school was going to participate in a sponsored day at Kauffman Stadium (the "K"), to watch a major league baseball game. Our family had previously attended a few Kansas City Royal's games, so Alex was somewhat familiar with the stadium layout. I thought that this could be a fun social activity for Alex. He was eager to go, so I volunteered to chaperone, as I knew that none of his support team was attending. I scheduled the day off work and was looking forward to a pleasant day. That morning the sun was shining, and the temperature was mild; perfect conditions for "school day at the "K.""

Alex and I arrived at school that morning to see the big, yellow buses already lined up and ready to chauffeur most of the 700 plus students to the game. We walked into the school gymnasium where organizers were staging groups of children to pair with their assigned chaperone. With no advance notice I was told that I would be responsible for five young boys, including Alex. I was a bit surprised that I had not been informed beforehand but thought, okay, no problem.

We arrived at the "K" well before game time and unloaded in the parking lot near the children's area that was separate from the stadium. The children's activity center offered a youth-sized, baseball field, where the children could run the bases, take a turn swinging the bat, visit with "Sluggerrr" the loveable lion mascot, or basically run around the area at free will. As I soon learned, the event was far too unstructured for such a large juvenile gathering. Alex was calmly hanging close to me, but my other four assigned high-energy kiddos were running throughout the crowd in every direction, as I desperately tried to maintain accountability for each of them.

During the chaos of that event, one of my hyperactive charges darted off to a large steel trash dumpster sitting in the parking lot and climbed up the attached seven-foot, side ladder, yelling, "I'm the king of the dumpster!" I finally caught up with him, talked him down and explained that it was too dangerous to play on the enormous garbage container. I hastily regrouped my wards and then two of the immature youngsters started a friendly fracas with each other that quickly escalated, and I immediately played referee, ending the scuffle before it got injurious. To make matters worse, directly after the scuffle, my fifth unruly child, who had been loud and obnoxious from the start, abruptly made an inappropriately rude comment to a well-endowed woman passing by who was wearing a skimpy, tight, white tank top and looked as if she was poured into her jeans. The rude quip included something about "jugs." I quickly apologized to the woman and her male partner, then explained to the child why his remarks were unacceptable. I stood there thinking, what have I gotten myself into? I demanded that each boy sit on the curb in the parking lot and not move until it was time to enter the stadium. As I was probing Alex about the boy's behaviors, I soon learned that they were all from the special-needs classroom. As that revelation sunk in, it occurred to me that I had been stuck with all the behaviorally challenged kids, and no one bothered to give me a heads up. I was livid! Just because I had a special needs child, I certainly was not qualified to deal with four additional out of control, immature boys in a "free for all" setting.

Once inside the stadium, the boys had assigned seats, so it became a little easier to manage them. They had no interest in the game, and they were continuously cutting up, but at least they stayed in their seats. Things started to settle down a bit as the players took the field, and just when I thought I may get to enjoy the game, the prepubescent girls sitting directly behind me began screaming at the top of their lungs, relentlessly spouting every baseball related phrase that existed, like an inebriated adult. I turned around and recognized that the loudest girl was the lead from the school musical that I had recently attended, where Alex was playing in the accompanying orchestra. I thought,

64

just my luck, I get stuck directly in front of the girl with the loudest projecting voice! A headache ensued and I prayed that the game did not go into overtime.

Halfway through the slugfest, Alex wanted something to eat. I gave him some money, and although I was not completely confident that he could recognize the correct change, at this point I didn't care. He walked down the steep concrete steps unchaperoned and disappeared under the stadium structure where the concessions were located. I was used to giving Alex freedom to explore, so I wasn't too concerned about his ability to navigate his way back. And I certainly was not going to leave my four hooligans alone for fear that they would be gone when I returned. Alex had been gone for a few minutes when out of nowhere one of the trip organizers saddled up to me and said, "You shouldn't be allowing the kids to go off by themselves." With my head pounding, the first comment racing through my head was, okay, where has your *ass*istance been all this time, and NOW you want to criticize? But that comment was kept internally. What I did calmly and confidently say was, "That boy is my son and I trust that he will find his way back just fine." Really, what could she say? She just turned around and left.

Mercifully, the baseball game ended after nine innings. With my head feeling like it was about to split open I could not have been happier to get on that bus and head home. Once we all disembarked at the school, I found the organizer who had chided me during the game and stated in a low and steady voice, "Do not EVER expect me to chaperone an off-site school event again." I explained to her that I was unknowingly encumbered with the responsibility to corral four additional special needs boys, with no advance warning, no assistance, and no guidance as to the boy's disabilities, quirks, or behaviors. She looked dumbfounded and sincerely apologized, saying that she had no idea. I gathered Alex, who thankfully had experienced a fun day, drove home and immediately downed two extra strength Tylenol.

During middle school Alex was still attending Adventure Club after school. Not that he couldn't be left home alone for the brief period between the end of school and my arrival home from work, but involvement in the club was an attempt to encourage and build social skills. The afterschool group played games and had free, unstructured social time. Alex came home one day, happy to have learned that a boy he had been playing table tennis with named Andy was also diagnosed with Autism. My heart was joyful. I was so eager for Alex to make a connection, as he was lonely and desperately needed a friend.

We had Andy over many times, and the two became "friends" - as much as two autistic people could emotionally and socially connect. They mostly played video games together, or independently watched each other playing the game. Andy would spend the night occasionally. Listening to their short and sporadic conversations was a completely different experience compared to the friendships I remembered as a kid, but these were two males, and I suppose females by nature can be chattier. Plus, society was completely different when I was growing up.

As a young child in the late sixties – early seventies, video games did not exist. I could not wait to go outside and play with the neighborhood children, engaging in all sorts of games, fort building, and exploration of the neighboring woods. My siblings and I would watch Saturday morning cartoons until 10:00 am, and then it was out the door, not to be seen again until the dinner bell rung. The bell was pulled from an old, metal, kid-sized pedal-car that was designed as a fire engine. It was attached to the outside of the house and the clanging could be heard from blocks away. When my mom rang that bell, her six children would run home from various locations in the neighborhood, like ants swarming to a piece of candy dropped on the ground.

The friendship between Alex and Andy was building through their eighth-grade year. However, due to school district mapping, the two buddies would be attending different high schools within the district. That left Alex starting high school with no real friends, once again. Knowing this, we requested a peer buddy during the IEP transition meeting, but that never came to fruition. I was informed that there were not enough monetary resources at the high school level to implement this request. Looking back, I may have been able to protest the denial with the "due process" procedure, but I did not have the energy to fight it, nor the funds to hire an attorney.

Throughout middle school Alex continued to utilize services funded through the Autism Project. He had mastered grade level "book work" related to social awareness. Now he needed to incorporate what he learned while participating in real-time community settings. Based on experience, it was impossible to preconceive every potential social scenario when outside of his normal daily routine. So, we hired a young man fresh out of college, Mr. Jason, to foster behavioral intervention while the two of them were taking part in public activities. Mr. Jason was extremely smart and kind, and Alex really liked meeting with him. Mr. J would pick up Alex and take him out to eat, teaching him how to order, pay his bill and leave an appropriate tip. Sometimes they would shop at a local bookstore, which offered the ability to practice appropriate dialogue with a clerk/cashier and ensure he received the correct change. They would also visit museums, where Alex would practice speaking quietly, as typically he spoke in a very loud voice. I recall constantly using a discreet hand gesture that alerted Alex to lower his volume.

After several years of bonding with Mr. Jason, Mr. J decided to advance his education and could no longer meet with Alex. No surprise. Like so many support personnel before him, paid professionals were only involved for a few years at best. Alex was extremely bummed that Mr. Jason was leaving and felt abandoned once more. This transition was taking place at a time in his life when he seriously needed some consistency with his external role models. Mr. Jason very sweetly offered to stay engaged with Alex via email (unpaid), but Alex still struggled with writing, and he did not respond when Mr. J reached out to him.

I expressed my concerns to the proprietor of the contracted agency we used, regarding the revolving door of support personnel and how it affected Alex's spiraling self-esteem. Out of true dedication, the owner, Mr. David started meeting with Alex in the interim, while he searched for a new employee to pair with Alex. Therapists hired by the agency came and went, and Alex never formed a strong bond with any of the new folks. But Mr. David always stayed connected while trying to identify support staff that was a good fit for Alex. Alex became comfortably familiar with Mr. David over the years and preferred visiting with him over anyone else. More than ten years later, Mr. David and Alex continue to meet in the community at least once a week. He's been a constant in Alex's life, which has been immensely crucial to his well-being. Mr. David was, and still is a gift sent from the universe.

And sweet Ms. Tammy, Alex's fourth and fifth grade teacher graciously continued to be in Alex's life after he left elementary school. She took on the role of Personal Care Attendant for about a year. On weekends, she and Alex would occasionally do fun things around Kansas City, as she administered her socially appropriate wisdom. The two of them attended a STOMP performance, which is a combination of percussion, movement, and visual comedy. I wondered if Alex would be able to handle a high-energy sensory event, but he had a great time. Thankfully he was learning how to control sensory intake and could mostly manage intrusions when needed.

Art continued to fuel Alex's enthusiasm. His eighth-grade class schedule was already filled with electives, consisting of orchestra and a technology course, which meant that art would be omitted this year. However, we soon learned that the school was offering an "early bird art class" that started before normal school hours. Alex was eager to attend the 7:00 a.m. class so every morning we headed for school in the darkness. By this time in my career, the workday began at 8:00 a.m. thus I had the luxury of an hour to calmly achieve my nine-mile commute from north of the river to midtown. In previous years, my normal rush-hour routine was racing down the highway, squeezing across the Missouri river bridge with thousands of other stressed-out motorists, jockeying lane positions to avoid the tortoise-like drivers, donning my jewelry when paused at a stop light, careening into my parking space, and darting into the building to arrive at my desk on time. It would have made sense to leave earlier allowing time for a more leisurely commute, but that objectively was not me. I needed every spare minute at home to get things done.

After sixteen years of working in labor divisions for the Postal Service, I took a leap of faith in the year 2000 and converted to management. I had accepted a temporary assignment in the Commercial Sales Division as an Account Manager and loved it. With the Stamp Fulfillment Division being a totally different animal regarding products and operations, I had quite a bit of learning ahead of me. I dug in and attempted to digest everything I could, from the many options of shipping software to over four hundred products and services, to the forty pages of different postage rates, to the stacks of publications on domestic and international rules and regulations, to the proper steps of direct mail marketing, to the competition's (UPS, FedEx) rates, rules, and regulations. If I was going to be a successful sales rep, I needed to understand what I was selling and who I was selling against.

Meeting new people, learning the ins and outs of many different industries, and providing solutions to meet the needs of businesses throughout the Mid-America District suited me well. Basically, I had been working toward a degree in business when I had to leave college behind. The hands-on education and multifaceted experiences as an Account Manager fed me new life. When a permanent position was posted, I applied and was accepted. Goodbye stagnant, gloomy cave! Goodbye to punching a time clock! I would however miss the people I worked with. They were, and still are a great group of folks.

The Sales position came with a flexible work schedule. A perk that enabled me to attend IEP meetings and school events during the day, take my kids to doctor appointments, and take care of my own health needs without having to use my sick leave or vacation days. I gave more than forty hours a week to my job but having the work-day flexibility was far more appealing. My Postal-issued laptop and cell phone meant that there was no place to hide if one of my accounts had a burning question or experienced negligent service in the evening or on the weekend. Some travel with overnight stay was required for regional and national sales meetings, as well as when visiting accounts on the opposite end of the district, which was a six-hour drive one way. Thankfully my husband, who I fully trusted to take exceptional care of our two boys, stepped up when I was out of town. I could not have successfully accomplished the duties of the position and gained subsequent job advancements without his reliability.

Alex continued to play violin throughout middle school, putting himself out there by performing solos that were critiqued for district ratings. I was so proud of his growth, as previously he was not good at handling criticism. Feedback from the judges was provided directly after his performances and he handled the comments without becoming upset. His private violin teacher held recitals periodically, and mine and Mike's family would attend to support him. Surprisingly, he was able to keep his anxiety contained before and during his performances. There were even a few times that he played at the nursing home where his grandmother Barbara, Mike's mom, was a patient in the Alzheimer's ward.

Barbara was a warm and loving grandmother in her coherent years. She doted over Alex, her only local grandchild for six years, until our second son was born. From the time Alex was a baby, she would call just about every Saturday afternoon, asking Mike if he and I were going out that night, and if she could have Alex? Even if Mike and I did not have set plans, we would find something to do. Barbara kept Alex overnight, then Mike and I would go to his parents' house for lunch the following day and spend most of our Sunday visiting with them. That respite was most welcomed and allowed me to get household chores completed on Sunday morning without a toddler under my feet.

As a teenager, Alex never expressed his emotions while he watched his beloved grandmother Barbara wither away in her last year, as each little stroke stole her ability to walk, then to speak, then to eat. For me, the process was gut-wrenching to experience. To walk into the nursing home cafeteria and see the once lovely, vibrant woman I knew slumped over her plate of unidentified puree, unable to hold her head up was enormously heartbreaking. We visited her in the Alzheimer's ward every Sunday. Through her facial expressions we knew that she still recognized us, but she had lost her ability to communicate. I cannot imagine how frustrating that must have been for a once very vivacious and engaging lady to now be silenced. She had managed a credit union for over thirty years and developed many friendly acquaintances. At age 72, she was forced into retirement because she was losing her ability to keep accurate financial records. She did not want to stop working, which in her mind meant relinquishing her connection to the world, but Alzheimer's was selfishly stealing her capabilities. Well over two hundred people attended her departing reception, as she reluctantly but gracefully said goodbye to coworkers and credit union members. To the unknowing, it was a joyous occasion. However, it was a somber event for those of us who knew what the future held.

By now, our youngest son was in second grade. There had not been any reports of unusual behavior to this point, so when Austin's teacher sent home a note stating that, "Austin spent forty-five minutes during regular class instruction circling a table in the back of the classroom" I thought, what the? The teacher assumed that Austin was completely disconnected from the ensuing lecture, but when he answered one of her questions during his canter, she was stunned that he had been actively listening. I was puzzled that up until now, former teachers had not shared any similar concerns related to classroom behavior. And because of Alex's diagnosis I had frequently watched Austin with a keen eye and never noticed any troubling characteristics. Be that as it may, with this new development it was clear that Austin was going to require assistance moving forward.

Being well immersed in the special needs community by now, I knew what steps needed to be taken. We had Austin evaluated at the Kansas City Regional Office and thankfully they ruled out Autism. But that still left us with no diagnosis. With no diagnosis, the school was unaware of how to build a plan to accommodate Austin's learning needs. So, we scheduled an evaluation at Children's Mercy Hospital which resulted in a diagnosis of "Pervasive Developmental Disorder – Not Otherwise Specified" (PDD-NOS). PDD-NOS falls under the umbrella of Autism Spectrum Disorder (ASD), so the school gave him an "Educational Autism" diagnosis in order to lay a foundation for developing an appropriate Individual Education Plan (IEP). Okay, so now we had two kiddos with special needs. This time I took it in stride.

Fortunately, Austin did not have extreme sensory conditions or behavioral issues when relating to his peers. No fights, no suspensions, no dark closets. After his regular education teacher consulted with the special needs coordinator, the school took away his standard chair and supplied a large, bouncy exercise ball instead, that allowed him to sit at his desk and remain in constant motion. Austin stayed on an IEP throughout the remainder of his school years but was always included in the regular classroom setting. In comparison, he was much easier to manage than Alex.

# Chapter 6.  High School

Academically, Alex had mastered Math and Spelling at grade level, so those IEP goals were removed as he ventured on to high school. His writing skills had advanced throughout junior high, but still needed work when the writing assignment required three paragraphs consisting of an introduction, body, and closing.  And if needed, modifications were included to lower the difficulty of writing assignments. An enormous amount of scholastic progress was made over the last three years and now only two educational goals were identified in his freshman IEP:

- Increase independent writing skills to five paragraphs – introduction, three paragraphs for the body, and one paragraph for the conclusion.

- Edit own written work for capitalization, punctuation, and complete sentence usage.

Special needs instruction utilizing the resource room was expected to be no more than 12% of Alex's day.  Although academics had improved, personal frustrations continued for Alex.  This was in part, due to lack of inference and correct interpretation of teacher and peer language, which resulted with the inability to emotionally connect with fellow students.  Alex took comments directed at him literally.  As stated in the IEP, staff was discouraged from using figurative language as it was not effective and mostly detrimental.  For example, if someone said, "That cake is calling my name," Alex could not infer that the person was craving cake and planned to eat a piece.  He would labor to interpret what that statement really meant, until it was explained.  How do you respond in conversation when you do not understand the true intent of a statement? Therein lies the obstacle of socially connecting. So, to promote social interaction a third goal was added to the IEP:

- Alex will join and continue to participate in an after-school activity 100% of the time.

When aggravated, inappropriate behaviors were still present and a plan for success was addressed in his IEP Behavioral Intervention Plan. The goal was for Alex to be able to follow directions even when feeling overwhelmed.

- Target Behaviors:
  - Use a respectful voice. Do not make unusual sounds such as growling and grunting.

- Support Provided by School:
  - Cool down pass to the drinking fountain to regain control over emotions.
  - One safe spot in the classroom with stress ball and comic books for 5-10 minutes.
  - If cannot calm in this short time, go to designated conference room used as a cool down area. May read or use sensory items.
  - Practice processing with a familiar adult and unfamiliar adult to help generalize this ability to all adults in charge at school.

- Alex will be accountable for:
  - Verbalizing the problem and possible solution before he can exit the cool down area.
  - Staying in assigned space.

Mike and I had met with Alex's new high school Case Manager Mr. Ryan and Alex's assigned counselor Ms. Julia. Mr. Ryan assisted Alex academically, keeping him on task and Ms. Julia compassionately helped Alex work through his emotions and confusions.

This would be Alex's first year riding a school bus with his typically developing peers. Until this point, he had been a car rider. Our home was a few blocks from the school district's bus lot, so he was first stop on the bus route allowing him to choose a seat up front near the driver. When I was young and living in New Jersey my mom drove a school bus. I remember riding with her one day as she was taking junior-high level children to school. One mean little boy had shoelaces in his hands and whipped them across the face of another young boy sitting directly in front of him, leaving painful red lines on his cheek. The picked-on child never flinched or turned around, but I could see that he fought back tears and painstakingly endured the ridicule that followed. I remember feeling extremely angry toward the aggressor and at the same time feeling empathy for the weaker boy, all the while wondering in frustration why the timid victim did not stand up for himself. That image is still vivid in my memory almost fifty years later. I was thankful that Alex was able to sit in the front of the bus to avoid potential bullies.

Starting freshman year in a new school building with no friends was certain to create challenges. The IEP team brainstormed ideas for social activities that would keep Alex engaged. He was offered a manager position with the high school baseball team. In the back of my mind, I quietly thought that the offer was not a good fit, but I wanted to let Alex try. Experience told me that Alex needed an activity with a little more structure. Besides, he hated strenuous physical activity and was only required to take one year of physical education in high school. The teacher's comments on his report card read, "Alex needs to put forth his best effort during the running activities," and "Alex often refuses to do the running activities." Back then, I did not understand his lack of motivation when it came to gym class. Being forced to run caused him anxiety and we eventually had to obtain a doctor's note to excuse him from running events. When I ask Alex about it today, he says, "I just didn't see any reason to be running."

Alex attended practices as baseball manager for a couple of weeks, however he received no guidance as to what his role was, nor was he introduced to the other managers or players. Support was not provided to ensure his success and he quickly became bored with the situation and quit the opportunity. "Back to the drawing board," um, I mean "now we must find another extra-curricular activity to promote social engagement."

With Alex's passion for painting and drawing proving to be therapeutic, he took an art class every semester in high school. At age fifteen we learned that a summer youth painting class was offered at the local Kansas City Art Institute and when we approached Alex with the idea of attending, he was immediately on board. After a conversation with the intake personnel regarding Alex's autistic characteristics and completing the required release form so that his diagnosis and behaviors could be shared with the teacher, we were ready to begin an exciting adventure. We could see the enthusiasm each day as he brought home new and inspiring artwork created throughout the summer. After eight weeks of experiencing the historical feel of the Art Institute (established in 1885), he was hooked. Alex was genuinely an old soul, and he knew deep down that the KC Art Institute was where he would attend college. Eventually, we would have to figure out how we were going to pay the exorbitant tuition for this private school.

Alex still enjoyed playing violin in the school orchestra, so during his freshman year I attended monthly meetings of the Orchestra Parent's Association (OPA), a non-profit entity that supported the North Kansas City High School orchestra. When freshman year concluded, I was asked to join the board as OPA Treasurer for the following year. I had some Excel skills, so I accepted the nomination. I was informed that I could be audited and was then handed an unorganized mess consisting of several hard copy binders that listed the names of over one hundred active and non-active orchestra students and their respective fundraising balances. Added to the stack was a general ledger of the checking account and a binder of OPA related documents. As I shuffled through the haphazard paperwork, I thought to myself, there is no way I'm going to track every entry for over eighty active orchestra students manually! I needed an easy way to document and share financial information.

After dissecting the muddled pile of previously kept books and now clearly understanding what information was important to have on demand, I created an Excel workbook with linked pages for an easy view of the general ledger's running balance, each student's running balance and a one-page worksheet that listed a snapshot of the total funds in each student's account. The orchestra director and board members were preparing for a trip to Disney World. With an abundance of fundraisers lined up, the Excel worksheets made my volunteer job as treasurer much easier when recording hundreds of entries.

After six months of selling popcorn tins, hosting taco dinners, working the Renaissance Festival, and selling donated roses at the school's orchestra concerts, we were financially able to allow every child that met the academic and attendance requirements to participate in the journey to Florida. As a chaperone I would have preferred to fly, but the budget called for two coach buses to drive eighty musicians along with the accompanying teachers and support team from Kansas City to Orlando. When late spring arrived, the adults loaded the buses with instruments, luggage, the kiddos, and plenty of snacks. We were all excited to head Southeast. The twenty-one-hour drive down was uneventful, and everyone was thrilled when we finally arrived at our enchanted destination. The orchestra performed at Magic Kingdom for part of one day, and the students had an additional two full days of free romping at the parks.

This time I knew in advance that I would have four young men that were developmentally delayed. I was familiar with all of them. Luckily, the youthful musicians were all well behaved - possibly because they were older and more mature than the rowdy pipsqueaks that I wrangled on the major league baseball trip in middle school. None of the boys were hyperactive or obnoxious. They were courteous, they stayed in a group, and they had a great time conquering the rides and taking lots of fun pictures.

On the last day, the students had a choice between Epcot and Animal Kingdom, and thankfully all the boys in our group agreed on Animal Kingdom. That park was a little more spread out with less sensory stimulation. There were no screaming babies in strollers, which Alex had a hard time tolerating. We rode the open-air safari bus around the park, watched an animated nature show, stopped to shop for souvenirs, and ate sweet treats from the vendors. The day's schedule called for a full day at the park, then by 5:00 pm all Kansas Citians boarded the buses for the twenty-one-hour ride back home. I had brought about fifteen DVDs to share between the buses to occupy the kid's attention and stave off boredom.

The trip back was going well until somewhere around Nashville, TN the air conditioning on our companion bus broke down and for some unknown reason, a replacement bus was not available. Imagine forty sweaty kids who spent all day running around an amusement park in the warm sunshine, then getting on the bus for a twenty-one-hour ride, with no circulating air. I'd wager that at least ninety percent of those teens had not taken a shower the previous morning. When we arrived home in Kansas City the following day, I climbed the steps of our sister bus to retrieve my DVDs and gagged when I was assaulted with a smell that resembled forty pairs of well-used gym socks, crammed in a tin box, and left out in the blistering sun. I was so grateful that we were on the bus with working air! I did not even want to think about how that choking aroma would have overloaded Alex's senses.

*High School Orchestra.*

Throughout Alex's high school years, the orchestra director and the parents who attended the orchestra association meetings were a joy to work with. The level of professionalism was refreshing compared to the PTA meetings of elementary and middle school. I spent a second year handling the finances as treasurer and then held the position of president during Alex's senior year. Being involved with the many fun activities and fundraisers, was a great way for me to stay connected with Alex and help him keep on track with his requirements to letter in Orchestra. There was a lengthy list of opportunities to play outside of high school. Alex volunteered to play at library teas, he traveled to the state's capitol building where the group performed in the rotunda, and he traveled throughout the school district performing with middle school and elementary orchestras. He was doing well and lettering each year in Orchestra, although one year I was unintentionally responsible for a hiccup in Alex's quest to attain his performance award.

As a Postal Service Account Manager, I was scheduled to attend our national trade show in Washington, D.C. I thought it would be a great opportunity for Mike and both our sons to experience our nation's capital. I booked their flights and later realized that Alex would miss a crucial upcoming orchestra performance...oops! Appreciatively, the orchestra director found another activity for Alex to complete that allowed him to qualify for his letter, thus bailing me out of my blunder.

When the Krahenbuhl family traveled using our own finances, our hotel price range was a Best Western or Super 8 equivalent. Because the yearly national trade show was a significant work-related event, the accommodations were typically higher-end hotels and undoubtedly not coming out of my pocket. Me, Mike, Alex, and nine-year-old Austin walked into the Washington, D.C. Hyatt hotel lobby to check in. There was a gleaming, grand piano in the foyer, an enormous, radiant crystal chandelier majestically hanging near a sweeping staircase of marble, and a breathtaking flower arrangement towering six feet tall, perched on a large, round antique marble table.

As the boys explored their surroundings on our way to the elevator, I wondered what would impress them the most. Would it be the astounding lobby? Would the lovely artwork on the walls capture their attention? Would they be amazed by the spacious room or the spectacular view of the city? When we entered our lovely room Alex and Austin quickly surveyed their digs where they would spend the next four days. From the bathroom, Austin uttered his first words since entering the hotel. He exclaimed, "Look at this, there are TWO toilet paper holders!" I had to smile and thought to myself, really, with all this grandeur THAT'S what impressed you? Mike and I got a good chuckle. With Alex's continued appreciation for art, he was able to enjoy the splendor of the building's artistry and architecture. Mike and the boys explored the city's historical monuments, as well as the Smithsonian complex and Ford's theatre where President Lincoln was assassinated. The historical experience of visiting our capital was more than a fair trade for missing an orchestra performance. In my opinion anyway.

By Alex's sophomore year it was clear that his number one difficulty was the inability to communicate appropriately, which resulted in a lack of social bonding and ability to cultivate relationships. He had recently joined the newly formed Hacky Sack Club at school. He would come home talking about the other club members and would refer to them as his "friends." I thought, great, he has found an activity and is making some connections. At the end of sophomore year Alex's 16th birthday was approaching. Traditionally, I had hosted my boy's yearly birthday party each May (Alex and Austin's birthdays are only four days apart) for relatives and friends. This particular year Alex expressed that he wanted a "school friends only" party. He said that he had invited a few school mates from the Hacky Sack Club to join him for food and games at the Brass Rail, a local billiards and arcade joint.

I offered to draft some invitations as I knew that the teenage memory could be short. Alex declined and said he had already spoken with his clubmates, and they verbalized that they were coming. I was not comfortable with Alex's lack of front-end preparation, but as requested, I reluctantly let him handle plans for his big day. As party day approached, I asked Alex on several occasions whether his invitees had confirmed their attendance. He was confident that his "buddies" would be there.

When the day came, Alex and I drove to the Brass Rail. We shot a few games of pool as we anxiously awaited the arrival of guests. It was the most heart-wrenching experience as a parent, when not one person showed. We ordered some food and Alex bravely kept his composure while we ate and shot a few more games of pool. I tried to keep the mood light, however on the drive home, he broke down crying. That heartbreaking memory is indelibly seared in my brain. I was just as crushed as he was and could not help but feel that I should have done more to ensure that at least one person showed. After that sad event, Hacky Sack Club vanished in the rearview mirror.

High school years were an emotional roller coaster. While going through Alex's tenth grade homework papers, I came across a journal and found this entry in Alex's handwriting.

*What Does Friendship Mean to You* – *"When people pick on you and make fun of you. People don't want to talk to you nor want to play with you. The only friends you have are yourself and no one else. Also, there aren't good people out there at all in this world."*

Realizing that my son desperately needed guidance, I researched the internet trying to find a solution for his inability to emotionally connect with peers. I discovered a social skills program called Circle of Friends. Here is a brief definition taken from the website:

*The 'Circle of Friends' intervention is aimed primarily at improving the inclusion of children with challenging behavior, disability, or personal concerns within mainstream schools. It works by gathering the student's peers in a circle of friendly support to help the young person with their problem solving. This approach can also be widely used with all students who are struggling to find support or friendship. Many schools have successfully tried the intervention with their students.*

I prepared a small packet of information related to this program, drafted a cover letter, and presented the concept to the school district's Superintendent, the district's Autism consultant, the school counselor and Alex's current personal life coach, Mr. Jason. Mr. Jason generously volunteered to facilitate the program on school grounds at no cost to the school district. The concept was well received, but as with any new program, the challenge was lack of funding to support its inception. I believe this program would have helped Alex tremendously during what were some of the toughest years of his young life.

A grant was written by school personnel to monetarily support a peer-to-peer social skills program, but time was needed for conceptualization, approval, and implementation. The program never came to fruition while Alex was attending high school. However, Alex received a letter in the mail from his high school during his freshman year in college. The letter informed him that the high school had finally implemented a social skills program and was inviting him to take part, as if he was still a high school student. This was too little too late. He had already moved on to a higher-learning institution. Being unaware that Alex no longer attended high school and sending an invite to a program that he so desperately needed back then felt like a slap in the face, especially after enduring years of emotional turbulence. I realized that the mistake was unintentional and took some comfort in knowing that other children would potentially benefit from the new social program.

The human need to be included and connect with people reminds me of a story in Melinda Gate's book called "The Moment of Lift." Melinda wrote about the charitable work that the Gates Foundation accomplished throughout the world. Within her publication she discusses another book written by a Catholic priest named Henri Nouwen called "Life of the Beloved." I was so moved by the profoundness of the following paragraph that I'm compelled to share it here.

> *Nouwen wrote: "In my own community, with many severely handicapped men and women, the greatest source of suffering is not the handicap itself, but the accompanying feelings of being useless, worthless, unappreciated, and unloved. It is much easier to accept the inability to speak, walk, or feed one-self than it is to accept the inability to be of special value to another person. We human beings can suffer immense deprivations with great steadfastness, but when we sense that we no longer have anything to offer to anyone, we quickly lose our grip on life."*

Personally, I think the poetic wisdom of the last sentence applies to everyone, not just people with disabilities. An example of this was my father-in-law. He was a private, quiet man. His lovely, vibrant, and social wife died ten years before he left this earth. As much as our family tried to engage him during those ten lonely years, the sad reality was that he gave up on his health and declined into non-social oblivion. God rest his gentle soul.

For Alex, high school years continued to be a struggle socially. While at work I received countless emails, phone calls and requests for in-person meetings to address behavioral matters. One incident resulted in Alex being kicked out of art class…art of all classes! The teacher had been busy helping another student. Alex did not understand the assignment and could not get her attention for help. In frustration, he took an Exacto knife and stuck the razor-sharp instrument in a linoleum block, then placed the block on the teacher's desk. She took that act as a personal threat to her safety and requested that Alex be permanently removed from her class. That was another trek to the school for an in-person meeting. During that meeting the art teacher conveyed that she was sensitive to Alex's actions because previously a former student pulled a knife on her. Listening to her talk throughout the meeting and observing her mannerisms revealed to me that she had a very high-strung demeanor. As it turned out, Alex was better off with his newly assigned art teacher, who had a calm and pleasant personality.

During Alex's sophomore year, his anxiety, depression, and agitated behaviors escalated to an unacceptable level. Weekly counseling sessions at school were reinstated to help Alex work through his roiling emotions, but those sessions alone were not enough support. We consulted with a psychiatrist at Children's Mercy Hospital hoping for a medicinal resolution. There were many drug options earmarked for depression and so began the guessing game of which one or combination thereof, would bring Alex out of the dark and calm his anger. The doctor initially prescribed the "drug of the day," a newly advertised treatment, but we soon learned that the side effects resulted with diarrhea. That drug was quickly dismissed. Over several months we cycled through many different medications, trying to find an effective solution without adverse outcomes.

During one of the medication trials, a discouraged Alex decided to take an abundance of pills at once; somewhere around twelve as he recalled. My husband and youngest son were not at home, so I had to think fast. I immediately told myself, okay do not panic, disconnect from your emotions, and focus on a solution. Luckily, I had a magnet on the refrigerator with a poison control number. I dialed the phone and a medical expert picked up right away. I asked if the specific drug that Alex had consumed could be safely vomited and they said, "yes." I disconnected the phone, approached Alex, and calmly said, "You have two choices. One: I can take you to the emergency room. They will pump your stomach and you will be on record as having overdosed, or Two: I can go to the store and get some Ipecac Syrup."

I explained to him that he would have to swallow the syrup and that it would induce vomiting. He chose the Ipecac, so off I went to the grocery store that was only three blocks away. Naturally every one of my nerve endings was burning with fright, but I never let Alex see that I was emotionally affected by his actions. I did not want him to think that he could invoke an emotional reaction from me, negatively influencing control over my psyche, that may have encouraged him to engage in future episodes. I swiftly arrived home, where Alex dutifully swallowed the Ipecac Syrup. Shortly thereafter, he was fertilizing the massive oak tree in the back yard. He was fine after purging, and mercifully we never had another instance of excessive pill-popping.

Agitated behaviors continued as we endeavored to find an effective drug that Alex could tolerate. Yet another school meeting was called to discuss a Communication Arts paper written by Alex that showed how dark his moods had become. Below is the assignment that was penned while we were desperately trying to find the medicinal silver bullet. Sixteen-year-old Alex wrote:

*"I chose to go to a normal school. That decision turned my life upside down. With that decision I have to take anti-depression medicine. That's why people hate me and I hate them. My parents helped me to decide on the decision to go to a normal school or an Autism school. Man, I'd picked the wrong thing in my life. Why? Why? I want to get out of here, it is killing me. I am rotting to the bone. I am becoming*

*a monster. Let me out of here. This is not school this is hell, hell and Satan is the teachers. I can see the fire coming from the bottom of the floor and the shackles on my ankles. I want to die; I want to die. It's a curse, it's a curse that I can't get out. Someone kill me, someone please kill me. I want to get out please. But this is a decision that I took and have to go through it. That's how it is and will stay that way."*

The tormented language and tone of the diatribe suddenly changes with the last two sentences, showing just how uneven my imbalanced teenager had become.

During this troubling time frame, the fallout at school fluctuated from serious to something as trivial as "Alex used the F word in a writing assignment." Okay, so I was born and raised in New Jersey. The F word is in our vernacular. And while I did a fairly, decent job of keeping my cursing tongue to a minimum, in the scheme of ALL THINGS currently being dealt with, writing the F word in an essay was at the bottom of my "uh-oh meter." In my opinion, that incident could have been handled by email versus requiring me to leave work for yet another in-person meeting. It seemed that each day there was another behavioral issue being presented to me, either by email or a direct phone call. While I wanted to know the problems being faced so that I could address them, it got to a point where I sighed with exhaustion when I saw an incoming email from the school counselor or glanced at the school's number on caller ID. Sophomore year was wearing me thin!

Alex's oscillating moods continued. One afternoon Alex and Austin were playing out in the front yard. Apparently little brother was irritating Alex, like any normal younger sibling. The next thing I knew, Austin was stumbling in the front door hopping on one foot complaining that Alex had body slammed him to the ground. Austin's ankle started to swell so we immediately applied ice. Fortunately, Austin did not appear to need any additional medical treatment…no cracked ribs, no busted lip, no blood. I did not raise my voice at Alex because

I had previously learned that increasing my volume only made him angry and mentally shut down. When in sensory overload he could hear my aggravated tone but was unable to process the words. I calmly explained the negative results of his behavior, articulating the typical parental line that "he was the older brother and should be setting a good example."

For days afterwards, ten-year-old Austin rolled around the house sitting on one of his dad's long skateboards, propping his black and blue ankle while using his hands to propel him from bedroom, to bathroom, to kitchen. When Austin rolled by, I said to Alex in a melancholy tone, "That is what you did to your little brother." I could see in Alex's body language that he regretted his harmful behavior. He never again physically injured Austin after that incident. Keeping calm, providing reason, and a clear outcome of consequences seemed to be an effective way to reach Alex. And by the way, we did offer crutches to Austin, but he thought it was much cooler to be scooting around on a skateboard.

Finally, after about a five-month battle of testing different medications we found a prescription drug that evened out Alex's mood. As a result, subsequent teacher reports stated that for the most part Alex was now demonstrating appropriate behavior and decision making. The school's lead counselor, Ms. Caroline decided that Alex no longer needed weekly sessions, if the staff was willing to consistently help him through troublesome situations and adhere to accommodations that were necessary for his success. Teachers were requested to provide:

- An alternative to making presentations in front of the class.

- Support during times of schedule changes – new semesters, altered bell schedules.

- Support during a change in routine – acceptance of tardiness in certain circumstances.

- Assistance with talking to or approaching his teachers or other staff about expectations that make him uncomfortable.

As per Ms. Caroline, this was a list of things that set him off in the past and would be best addressed as they took place within the school day instead of once a week in a counseling session. Once again, we were back on track and fixated on academics instead of behaviors.

Of course, grades were always on the radar. For the most part Alex remained focused on his assignments. However, when he needed help and could not find it on his own, I would step in to assist. Below is one of many intervention emails sent to Alex's high school Case Manager.

*Dear Mr. Ryan,*

*Below are Alex's grades to date. As you can see, he is failing Algebra II. Alex has tried Academic Outreach and states that "no one helped me." Please let me know what other options are available, so that Alex can pass this class. Alex has an hour and a half open on Wednesdays during Advisory. Is there a student that is proficient with Algebra and possibly needing A+ hours that can tutor Alex? Alex is also willing to stay after school if that is an option. I look forward to finding a resolution that will enable Alex to get through the remaining weeks of the school year.*

As always, Mr. Ryan came through with guidance and a remedy that allowed Alex to end the year with a passing grade. Another emotional disaster averted! Alex could not have a failing grade if he wanted to qualify for the A+ scholarship that aided in college tuition. And with his grade point average teetering on the brink, his anxiety was rising. He still had his heart set on attending the Kansas City Art Institute.

With Alex being proficient on the violin, the guitar was an easy transition for him. We owned several guitars as Mike was a collector with a technical mind for instruments, but not very skilled at playing the guitar. His musical competency was trumpet in high school band. On his own, and without any guitar lessons Alex started playing Mike's guitars. During sophomore year Alex learned that the high school had an after-school guitar club. Finally! A club where Alex could participate. His taste in music was old school, Delta Blues. His guitar style modeled musicians like Robert Johnson, Elmore James, Hound Dog Taylor, and the many other bluesmen from the 30's, 40's, and 50's. Finger picking is what he gravitated toward and played at home.

Alex was hopeful that the high school guitar club would learn to play half-century old songs from the blues genre, but it was impossible to find other sixteen-year-olds with an interest in music that had very little fame in its day. Alex still participated in the weekly guitar club meetings and played current popular rock songs in the group's year-end concert. It was a proud and joyful moment as I sat in the audience watching him jam with the other musicians.

Part of Alex's musical influence may have started when he was five. It was 1997 and a young blues prodigy named Kenny Wayne Shepherd had just released his second album. The band was touring and set to perform at an intimate club in Kansas City. I desperately wanted to attend the concert; however, Mike was working evenings and the show was scheduled on a weeknight. With a special-needs child, asking the neighborhood teenager to be responsible for your unpredictable preschooler was out of the question, so I took Alex with me. The band was positioned at ground level on what was typically the dance floor. There was no stage at this venue that usually rocked out to a disc jockey. There was no barrier between the musicians and the crowd. Alex and I stood two rows back from the band, barely three feet away from the artists. I had a spectacular line of sight, but my three and a half footer had trouble with the view. I grabbed a bar stool, stood Alex on top and held on to him for stability. We spent the evening enjoying one of the best modern blues guitarists in the mid-west. An event that we both vividly remember to this day.

Alex's iPod was loaded with old blues songs that helped him calm during episodes of sensory overload. He always kept the iPod in his backpack. During his sophomore year he left his backpack in the classroom while he went to discuss an issue with his counselor. He did not immediately realize that some young thief had helped themselves to his iPod, never to be seen again. Of course, he was upset, as by now music was a crucial tool that Alex used to calm himself. Obviously, no one fessed up, so we had to purchase another iPod and reload his music. Albeit expensive, this was an opportunity to teach him about the responsibility of his personal property. The experience culminated with me attempting to teach him the lesson of "trust with caution." A very broad concept that Alex had a hard time grasping, and for me, was tricky to convey. Honestly, how do you generically identify an untrustworthy person without some degree of stereotyping? For most of us trust is an instinct. An instinct that Alex lacked.

There was no shortage of mean and deceitful kids in Alex's very diverse high school of sixteen hundred students. One Friday on a chilly fall evening, our family attended a high school football game. I was working the concession stand, raising money for the orchestra, and Mike, Austin and Alex were hanging out at the game. After the game was over Alex was talking with a male student in the shadows of the three-story brick school building. I do not know if he was lured there, but Alex certainly misinterpreted the danger of this hoodlum. The troubled student punched Alex several times in the face, knocked his glasses to the pavement, and stomped them into a mangled, irreversible mess.

I just happened to be coming around the building at the end of this scuffle and the boy ran off. I was taken aback, not knowing what I should do when Mike turned the corner. I quickly explained what happened and then I hurried into the school to find an authority for some guidance. I came upon a room with an open door where the principal and another staffer were having a conversation. I explained what had happened hoping for some direction, but they just looked at me with blank stares as if to say, that is not our wheelhouse, and you are interrupting our conversation. They offered no direction and I quickly surmised that they would be of no help, so feeling let down I quickly left and returned to the scene of the crime.

Thankfully, my husband had the common sense to find a police officer who was still on the grounds. Mike explained the situation and Alex gave a description of the perpetrator. The officer said, "Oh, we know who this kid is; we'll look for him." The officer left in his patrol car, cruising the neighborhood and shortly afterward apprehended the suspect. Apparently, this juvenile delinquent was well known for causing trouble.

The following Monday I met with a school administrator and was encouraged to press charges. I naively only wanted the boy to be responsible for Alex's new glasses, but I was informed that it would be best for the child to be placed in the system for services. Well, I was certainly on board for an attempt at reform. I then pondered that this child may have had a horrible living environment with bad role models, and I agreed to take legal action with the hopes that the troubled young man would get the help he needed.

I never received any follow up from the school regarding the wayward child and naturally we were out the expense of having to purchase another pair of glasses. Mike and I tried to understand from Alex what caused the situation to spiral out of control, but he became irritated and shut down every time we attempted to bring up the episode. Possibly out of embarrassment or not wanting to relive the traumatic incident. We could only hope that he learned a lesson in how to interpret negative body language and verbal tone, and why the encounter escalated.

After a long battle with Alzheimer's, Alex's beloved grandmother Barbara sadly passed away at the end of his junior year. Being informed by medical professionals that she was close to passing, Mike and I stayed by her bedside late into the evening. Her body movements, although extremely limited revealed that she was still reacting to our voices, and we were able to share our final thoughts. Alex handled the funeral without tears or any discernable sadness and was able to recall many happy instances from his childhood. I frequently referred to Mike's parents as June and Ward Cleaver, as in my eyes they were the perfect parents, never publicly arguing or treating each other with disparagement. We missed my mother-in-law dearly, as she was such an enormous part of our lives.

Most kids Alex's age, now seventeen, were finding summer jobs. Any entry level task that required rapid-paced production like fast food or had direct contact with the consumer such as a convenience or grocery store was not conducive for Alex. These types of chaotic environments caused too much sensory stimulation. With the emotional maturity of a fourteen-year-old he was not ready to handle a job interview on his own. Luckily, through an online application and with parental push, Alex was able to secure a volunteer position at the local library where he spent a few days each week throughout the summer reshelving books using the Dewey Decimal System. The quiet, non-chaotic environment of a library was the perfect fit. Although there was no pay, the job experience was an invaluable lesson in responsibility. Tackling the stacks of reading materials at a comfortable pace gave him purpose and a feeling of accomplishment at the end of his shift.

During high school assemblies Alex continued to experience hearing sensitivity. Although, unlike in elementary school, he was no longer lying down on the gym floor to tolerate the high-energy event. He would attend the dynamic celebration for a brief period and then leave or would basically skip the excitement and go to his designated safe spot to work on homework. By twelfth grade, and with the right medication, Alex's erratic emotions had smoldered and thankfully, behavioral issues seemed to greatly decrease.

Taking theater and stage design classes as a senior was a perfect way for Alex to lend his artistic talents to scenery creation, as well as play violin in the orchestra pit of the theatrical performances. He was comfortable with the friendly, patient male teacher and his fellow classmates. In the spring of his senior year, the theater group took a trip to California, and of course I tagged along to ensure that Alex's needs were met. The agenda included a visit to Venice Beach, a tour of Paramount Studios, free time in Hollywood walking through Grauman's Chinese Theater and Madame Tussauds wax museum, a full day in San Diego and two full days at Disneyland.

We arrived at LAX airport around noon on a gorgeous, sunny, Los Angeles day, and then immediately bussed to Venice Beach. Once there, the Kush Bud hawkers lining the boardwalk were boasting the quality of their cannabis, tempting anyone within earshot to purchase their recreational bliss. We quickly steered the kids to the sandy beach and spent the remainder of our afternoon unwinding along the Pacific Ocean.

There were artists (and I use that term loosely) spread about on blankets attempting to sell their creations. I know that beauty is in the eye of the beholder, but I stood there contemplating why anyone would part with their hard-earned money on a rudimentary, cross-shaped palm leaf, appearing as if fashioned by a preschooler. My facial expression must have revealed my thoughts, as one of the other chaperones mumbled under her breath to me that the beach dwellers were all living on trust funds. I'm not sure how she knew that, and maybe it was just a sarcastic assumption. Nonetheless, their glassy eyes, disheveled appearance, and obvious absence of hygiene suggested a life lacking motivation.

While the beach was an interesting experience, we were all looking forward to the following day in San Diego. We piled on the bus at 8:00 am in Los Angeles and headed south. First stop on our agenda was the San Diego Zoo. The zoo was phenomenal.

Every single animal looked incredibly healthy and the landscape, that never saw temperatures below freezing was gorgeously dressed in a variety of brightly colored flowers and abundant greenery. The weather was mild and sunny, and the day progressed perfectly until we were leaving the park that afternoon. The entire theater group was staged at the exit of the zoo waiting for our bus. I was talking with some of the chaperones and Alex was standing near a group of kids about thirty feet away.

Suddenly Alex dropped like a rock, and laid motionless on the concrete sidewalk, frightening everyone. We were all stunned! As my mind raced and my pulse quickened, I thought, oh my god, is he having a stroke? A heart attack? Did he crack his head on the pavement? Everyone was frozen in disbelief and looked at me to take some sort of action.

I rushed over to Alex and saw that his eyes were open and there was no blood. That was a good sign. Confused beyond measure, I asked Alex if he was okay. He said, "Yes" and he started to sit up. I asked, "What happened?" He told me that an enormous, angry horsefly had buzzed his head and it freaked him out and down he went. He finally regained his composure and made it to his feet. I then got to experience the humiliation that Alex had endured his entire life, as the adults just blankly stared in confusion and the pack of girls from our group started giggling and whispering among themselves. I completely understood why an amplified horsefly would drop Alex. Those beastly San Diego horseflies were five times bigger than the ones in the midwest. I gave a brief explanation of Autism to whoever would listen, but the unknowing adults showed no understanding of his disability. And being that we were at the end of a four-hour, feet-numbing trek on asphalt they really did not seem to care, so we modestly held our heads high and carried on into the afternoon.

Next stop on the San Diego agenda was a tour of the USS Midway, a decommissioned Naval aircraft carrier.

For the historically minded individual, this floating museum was intriguing and educational. And although I could not make sense of the overwhelming instruments, levers, buttons, and toggle switches, I embraced the journey as we squeezed through tight doorways, climbed metal rung ladders exposing new levels, and stood motionless on the enormous deck, imagining the skill and precision needed to land a plane in such a short distance.

Up until this point in our day the weather was sunny, but just as we were about to board our small-scale ship for a cruise of the San Diego Bay, it started to drizzle. For the entire one-hour, gloomy, overcast voyage, we were tossed about by waves and pelted in the face with cold rain, preventing us from seeing the coastline and other docked military ships, that the tour guide attempted to highlight via a muffled, indiscernible speaker. Not the best experience, but I amused myself by silently singing the Gilligan's Island theme song.

The next two days would be spent at Disneyland. The theater production of Aladdin was musically entertaining and meeting the cast afterwards revealed an enthusiastic group of actors that clearly enjoyed their job. For us older folks, it was a nice break to be off our feet for an hour. While touring the costume workshop we watched the workers wash and restyle the well-known Disney character wigs. There were racks of elaborate dresses for Jasmine, Snow White, Sleeping Beauty, and the like. An entire bustling division was devoted to preserving character costumes.

As expected, the amusement park atmosphere was electric with crying babies, squealing toddlers, darting teenagers, stimulating rides, flashing lights, touchy-feely-life-sized-in-your-face Snow White, Goofy and Mickey, combined with the monotony of "It's a Small World After All" relentlessly playing through speakers over and over and over. By noon on day two, Alex had enough sensory input. One more minute of intrusion would have sent him over the edge. Again, I could not leave the kids that I was chaperoning at the park by themselves. Who was going to ensure that they arrived at our designated gathering spot at the appropriate time to board our bus at the end of the day? I had no idea where the rest of the group was as everyone was dispersed doing their own thing, and no adult I attempted to reach answered their phone.

Feeling overwhelmed Alex was desperate to leave and assured me that he would be fine taking the tram back to our hotel. Since he was quite comfortable with exploring on his own, off he went by himself.

I was proud that he felt confident enough in unfamiliar surroundings to make his way alone. Although my nerves were a little jumbled until several hours later when I finally received a call from him saying that he had stopped to eat at a burger place and then safely returned to the hotel. A wave of relief allowed the grip on my lungs to loosen. Now I could keep tabs on the remaining young students without being distracted. Early the next morning, we boarded our flight home completely depleted of energy but without incident. The trip was a successful, grand finale to Alex's high school years.

Throughout senior year Alex worked hard to maintain grades and complete the necessary requirements to obtain Missouri's A+ scholarship. The scholarship paid tuition for eligible graduates of participating schools who attended a two-year community college after high school. Among the GPA and attendance requirements, Alex needed to achieve fifty hours of tutoring to qualify. His coordinating skills were not his best attribute, so I spoke with school personnel to find the appropriate fit for Alex's abilities. He did well in History and earned some tutoring hours by assisting high school classmates with their history homework. By the end of the school year, he still needed thirty hours of tutoring and time was running out. After several conversations, emails, and consistently pestering Alex's school case manager, I received notification that the A+ coordinator had finally found an opportunity for Alex. He was scheduled to support the summer-school teacher of fifth-grade orchestra students by helping the amateur musicians tune their instruments. The summer-school building was ten miles from our house, in the opposite direction of my work, adding twenty miles to my commute, but we made it happen. By six weeks into the summer, fifty hours of tutoring was on the books. Alex was now officially qualified for the A+ scholarship.

Because constant stimulation during the school day exhausted Alex's brain, and he was working incredibly hard to meet graduation requirements, he certainly did not have extra energy to research additional scholarship applications. Never having been through the scholarship experience myself, I innocently thought, how hard can it be? Certainly, I should be able to fill out a few forms. I recalled one middle school teacher telling me, "There's no need to worry, there is plenty of scholarship money out there for the disabled." Over the next few months, I spent weekends scouring the scholarship website (fastweb.com) for funding opportunities related to Autism or developmental disabilities, but disappointingly found none...zero. I was most definitely misled. The selections on Fastweb were slim for my son, as it was clear that most were looking for the over-achiever. After drilling down through hundreds of listings and weeding out the offers where Alex met initial qualifications, I electronically completed and sent ten lengthy submissions. By then I was mentally exhausted with no more effort to give. Finding grant money for college was not an easy task while working full time and raising two kids on the spectrum. But every little bit helped, and I was appreciative that Alex was awarded one $500 scholarship.

Since Alex was already acquainted with the Kansas City Art Institute (KCAI), he had determined that KCAI was where he wanted to further his knowledge of art history and creative technique. But how could we afford this very expensive private school? Although the A+ scholarship would have covered his tuition to a two-year community college, Alex was adamant that the Art Institute was his choice. I was familiar with the local community college campuses since I had taken classes at three of the four locations. I knew that one of the campuses had recently built a lovely new art center, because I drove passed the campus frequently. I convinced Alex to tour the new art center with me, but he was not impressed. The contemporary grounds did not have the same historic vibe that spoke to my kiddo's old soul as did the Art Institute, with its nineteenth-century stone buildings.

But first things first. Alex needed to be accepted by the Art Institute. They required a minimum SAT score of 20 and Alex's score was 19. Alex, Mike, and I met with the admissions staff where they interviewed Alex and reviewed his portfolio of artwork that he had accumulated over the years. They must have foreseen potential (or dollar signs) because they were willing to disregard his lower SAT score. However, before they approved his admission, they asked Alex to create a set of three small art pieces that were related to each other in some way. Alex agreed and by the time we reached our parked car, he already knew that he would paint the front view of a man playing guitar, a man playing a drum set, and a man walking away with a guitar slung over his back.

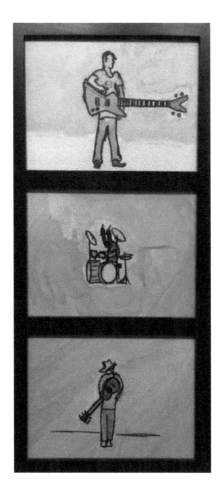

*First Art Institute assignment.*

A week later, Alex presented the requested artwork to intake personnel, and they agreed to accept him into the Art Institute. Alex was elated and we were quite relieved to get over that hurdle. Now, to figure out how we were going to pay tuition. Luckily, KCAI provided Alex with a scholarship that reduced his tuition by forty percent. We financed a small portion, and the remainder was made in large monthly payments. The next four years were very lean as we pinched our pennies and skipped vacations.

At the end of Alex's senior high school year, Mike, Grandma Mary (my mom), and I attended a ceremony specifically to honor the students that were accepted to a college or university. The principal acknowledged each child's awarded scholarships and named the school where they would continue their education. The moment after they announced that Alex would be attending the Kansas City Art Institute, that the Institute had provided a scholarship, that he qualified for the A+ scholarship, and that he had additionally secured a $500 scholarship, there was a hushed buzz throughout the crowd. I was hopeful that the many teachers, counselors, and administrators who had spent countless hours supporting Alex emotionally and academically felt a sense of accomplishment, knowing that their hard work and dedication over the last four years had paid off. When Alex was little, I never dreamt that he would have had the ability to attend college. We could not have been prouder!

Alex turned eighteen in the last month of his senior year. Having attended conferences that explained what happens to a parent's rights when your child becomes a legal adult, I knew Mike and I would need to apply for legal guardianship. Otherwise, we would have had no rights to view Alex's medical information and assist with making any health decisions if a serious incident occurred. Alex was not yet emotionally mature enough to make those kinds of decisions without adult input. He still experienced high anxiety when placed under pressure.

As explained by the Special Needs Planning Center, legal guardianship required a court appearance with a sitting judge to conduct a hearing. We hired an attorney to handle the paperwork and court proceedings. By law, Alex was assigned a court appointed attorney to advocate for him and ensure that we were not illegally railroading him against his will. We already knew Alex was on board with guardianship or we would not have wasted time moving forward with the process. Nonetheless, we had to follow legal procedure.

The hearing was simple and quick, lasting a total of maybe fifteen minutes. Sitting on the stand, I was asked to confirm my relationship to Alex, to convey my intentions of guardianship, and explain my thoughts concerning Alex's lack of self-advocacy. Then Mike took the stand and echoed my sentiments. Next, Alex took the stand. His attorney explained what guardianship meant and asked him if he had any objections. Alex said, "No." We breezed through the entire process. The judge gave his approval, and we were on our way in what seemed like a blur.

As Autism is a lifelong disability, at age eighteen Alex became eligible to apply for Social Security Assistance, a small monthly stipend that would help pay for his school cafeteria account, monthly city bus pass, and additional art supplies needed for class projects. He certainly did not possess the wherewithal to hold a job and tackle higher education at the same time. I had heard fellow parents of autistic children remark that acceptance into the Social Security system would not be a pleasant process and they were correct.

I scheduled an appointment for me and Alex to meet with a social security intake employee. To ensure that I was prepared, I armed myself with a copy of Alex's official diagnosis from the state and our guardianship document embossed with the official county court seal. Alex and I arrived at the small satellite office and waited in the lobby for our turn to present our case. When our name was called, we entered a cramped cubicle and sat across the desk from an old, unsmiling man with a look on his tired face that screamed, "I do not want to be here!" I thought, okay, be polite and do not set this man off. He has direct control over our fate.

I kept my tone cordial as I shared copies of our documentation, anticipating that our encounter would go smoothly. The gaunt, gray-haired man started asking me questions to complete the necessary forms laid out on his desk. When he came to the question that asked what we spent on groceries, he automatically assumed that our food bill for a family of four was only $400 a month and started to write down that amount. I guess if we ate hot dogs and beans every day that may have been accurate, but we ate healthier meals. And unfortunately, healthy food in our society costs more money.

When I told him that our monthly grocery bill was closer to $800, he became agitated and condescending. At that moment my perception of him believed that he was shamefully accustomed to intimidating people with disabilities. He began talking about social security taxes and snidely explained what they were, with a tone that indicated I was some type of degenerate. Now offended, I countered with a defensive attitude and said, "I know what social security taxes are, I've been paying them for the last forty years." He was taken aback by my directness, and I'm guessing that he was used to brow-beating people that had a subdued demeanor.

It was obvious that the man was jaded from years of dealing with people who were surviving on government dollars, but that certainly was not our long-term intention. The social security supplement was to subsidize Alex until he was able to hold a job sufficient to support himself. I was dismayed that we were treated like scourge and had a gut feeling that he would not submit accurate information in our favor. But as we were leaving, I took the high road and stuck my hand out with a smile. He hesitated to shake my hand, but after a few beats he relented.

When I arrived home, I searched the internet for our state capital's social security office phone number in Jefferson City. I immediately called and a pleasant lady answered the phone. I respectfully explained that we had been treated rudely by "Mr. Cranky" in the Kansas City office and that I felt he was going to file inaccurate information in our application. Amazingly, she said that she would handle my case from the state office. I surely was not expecting that outcome but was immensely grateful. I never had to deal with Mr. Cranky again. My guess is that it was not the first time she had heard his name in a negative light.

It took several months for the state's decision to arrive via mail, but eventually Alex was approved and successfully entered in the social security disability system. I felt very fortunate that Alex was accepted in the first round, as I have known other families with young autistic adults that were initially denied and had to fight through appeals.

# Chapter 7. College Years

As with most college class scheduling, class times varied during the day and evening. With Mike and I both working and Alex not yet able to drive, we needed to figure out transportation to and from school. Hiring a private driver was way beyond our financial reach.

Mike researched several city bus schedules originating in Kansas City North and mapped out a route. The nearest bus stop to our home was a simple two-block walk. Once on the bus Alex rode seven miles to downtown Kansas City, where he arrived at 8th & Main, which marked the end of that bus route. From 8th & Main, Alex walked another five blocks to 11th & Walnut to transfer bus routes. From 11th street he caught the bus heading south for an additional five miles. An hour into his trip Alex exited the bus and walked another four blocks to the KCAI campus. The same routine was followed for his commute home.

Initially, Mike and Alex made several advance runs together so that Alex felt confident that he could make the journey on his own. And for the next four years our budding artist traveled to and from school using the Kansas City Metro bus system, enduring single digit temperatures, snow-packed sidewalks, blustery winds, dreary rain, and extreme heat conditions during summer classes.

On one gloomy spring day, Alex was waiting at a bus stop when the weather turned dangerous. Radar indicated that a tornado was barreling down in his direction. Luckily, an older and wiser gentleman who was also waiting at the stop kindly directed Alex to a retail store where they took shelter. Just before the twister reached where they were hunkered down, it skipped up into the sky and disappeared. Hazard avoided!

Throughout those four years of riding the city bus, there were events that tested Alex's resolve to keep his composure. There were frequent, hygienically challenged passengers who severely neglected their personal care sending Alex's sense of smell into overdrive. Then there was the mentally imbalanced young woman who loudly talked to herself while gesturing with jerky hands, completely unaware of the world around her. On one frightening occasion an uproar arose when a disturbed man became hostile toward another patron, and angrily wielded his knife, displaying threatening behaviors. The bus was stopped, the police were called, and within minutes the offender was hauled off the bus and taken away. Another sticky situation occurred when a young mother with a small child wearing an arm cast felt that she was entitled to sit in the handicap seating area, and an older, ill-tempered man also sitting in that area apparently thought otherwise. An argument ensued that was still going strong when Alex reached his stop and quickly exited. Alex eventually grew accustomed to the drama, as it were, of inner-city bus commuting.

At the beginning of freshman year Alex and I were introduced to Ms. Kathy, the disabilities coordinator for the Art Institute. I was elated to learn that she was taking the lead with Alex to ensure that his school needs were met and to address anxiety issues as they arose. Ms. Kathy established a weekly standing meeting with Alex in her office that allowed him to discuss his fears, frustrations, and concerns; and in turn allowed her to direct him to the appropriate resources.

Early in the opening semester, Alex came home stressed out and unable to verbalize to me what was going through his head. I asked Ms. Kathy for a meeting, hoping to identify the triggers and provide some assistance. Even though we had legal guardianship and were paying the tuition, Ms. Kathy was unable to discuss anything related to Alex (without his presence) before he signed a release form. I understood protecting his privacy, but when you are the legal guardian, in addition to the one footing the bill, you can't help but feel a little slighted when you are procedurally shut out. To remove this obstacle, we coached

Alex through the online signature process of the release form and then Ms. Kathy and I were legally allowed to collaborate. Turns out that Alex had extreme difficulty accepting constructive criticism of his work from peers, to the point that he yelled at the teacher and stormed out of the classroom. It was very hard for him to distinguish between genuine constructive comments and someone ripping on his work. Ms. Kathy had to explain Alex's disability to the teacher, who thankfully understood, and allowed Alex to return to class the following day.

Ms. Kathy was a gem. She loved her job, bestowed an enormous amount of compassion, and greatly cared about the student's success. Ms. Kathy refreshingly imparted her wisdom based on previous decades of working with special needs students at the high school level. I received periodic emails from her as we teamed up to ensure that we were both in sync with Alex's emotional status.

Alex was still struggling with writing assignments causing him frustration and grief. I relayed to Ms. Kathy, "Alex has always had difficulty with writing assignments resulting with a self-defeated attitude even before he begins." Ms. Kathy always imparted her heartfelt expertise and was well versed with the delicate balance of expectations versus limitations. After meeting with Alex that day she wrote to me in an email, *"I hope Alex is ok. I felt terrible that he was so sad. He is experiencing what many freshmen feel. Freshman year is a huge adjustment, even for students who don't face his challenges and many of them do not have the forethought to ask for help. I would really like for him to bring his paper in tomorrow morning, but I don't want to push too hard."* Her communication allowed me to gently prime Alex that evening to bring his paper to their morning meeting. Working in tandem with Ms. Kathy helped to soften the delivery of demands.

The university professors continuously looked to Ms. Kathy for her guidance. To prevent Alex from dropping a class because of a difficult writing assignment, she approved a teacher request that allowed Alex to present a paper orally, one-on-one as an appropriate accommodation.

Assuredly, Ms. Kathy was a busy lady with around twenty-five percent of the Art Institute's students' having some degree of learning disability. During a journalistic interview she noted that, "*Art and design students are a special population. At a typical four-year institution, you'd find that 12 to 13 percent have learning disabilities. We run twice that.*" clarifying that "*learning disabilities are not correlated with IQ. Art students tend to be very right brained, and some of the same things that make a person creative manifest themselves in challenges such as dyslexia. My job is to get them to believe in themselves and what they can do.*"

Ms. Kathy used the animated classic "Dumbo" to encourage her student's confidence. When Dumbo the big-eared elephant and his little mouse friend wake up in the top of a towering tree, the mouse realizes that Dumbo can fly. The furry pocket-sized companion convinces Dumbo to fly again, using the deception of a "magic feather" to build his confidence. When performing in the circus, Dumbo tries the flying stunt, but he accidently releases the feather, losing his confidence and spirals into a nosedive. The mouse frantically reveals that the feather was never magical, that Dumbo could fly all along, and in the nick of time Dumbo pulls up, avoiding a crash landing. Ms. Kathy provided support for her students until they realized that they could fly without a feather.

When teachers appeared to be too busy to interrupt, Alex was intimidated and afraid to seek assistance. Being kicked out of art class in high school may have been one catalyst for his apprehension. Over the semesters, Ms. Kathy coached him to better advocate for himself. Always keeping me informed, she shared in an email, "*When I asked Alex why he had not brought the writing assignment in for me to help him he said it was because I am always so busy. Well, I am busy, but I don't want him to think I am ever too busy to help him. I will find the time. I'm finally getting a real assistant because I am so busy and worry about finding enough one-on-one time. I think Alex will like the man I am hoping to hire.*" Ms. Kathy was always thinking in terms of what was good for her students.

To retain his scholarship for sophomore year, the Art Institute required a 3.0 grade point average. At the end of freshman year Alex had a 2.99 GPA, slimly missing the target by a meager one one-hundredth of a percent. The letter we received in the mail stated that he no longer qualified for discounted tuition. Again, Ms. Kathy came to our rescue with the appropriate guidance, as we worked through the appeal process, completing online forms and crafting supporting documents. After consideration, an exception was granted. Huge exhale! One year down, three to go.

Although Alex was gradually adapting to college life, he still lacked the ongoing ability to advocate for himself. During his sophomore year he took a ceramics class on campus that was held throughout the six-week winter break. After a week of attending classes, Alex informed us that he was going to drop the course. That meant fifteen hundred bucks down the drain! When we asked Alex why, he said that the classroom was too cold. We asked Alex to find a custodian to turn up the heat. Alex could not bring himself to ask because his anxiety overwhelmingly escalated with the thought that he would be bothering someone for his benefit. I emailed Ms. Kathy (who was enjoying holiday break) explaining the situation and asked if she could contact a custodian to increase the room's temperature. She got right on it and the problem was resolved. As simple as the resolution was, unfortunately, Alex would just as soon walk away from a situation that caused anxiety instead of advocating for his needs.

Alex still grappled with writing assignments and used the resource room where student-provided assistance was available. Late one evening, he was working on a paper and asked one of the attendants for help. The student looked at his work and asked him if he was illiterate. Obviously, this student had no expertise with disability and most likely did not realize that his comment was inappropriately damaging. With his self-esteem now crushed, Alex remained in a low mood for about a week until Ms. Kathy identified another schoolmate who helped Alex without assigning a label. Alex was smart, but his neuro disability affected the part of his brain that inhibited the proper articulation of written language and oral conversation. As I was watching a late-night television show recently, I heard Hannah Gadsby, an autistic comedian, proclaim "How can I be so intelligent and struggle to leave any proof?" That insightful statement is the essence of how high-functioning, intellectual autistic people are misperceived.

As months came and went, Ms. Kathy and I relentlessly worked through typical issues that arose, ranging from the daunting software learning curve in graphic arts class to propping Alex's teetering self-esteem. As project deadlines started to slip, Alex needed a reminder that the studios were open late into the evening and was encouraged to make use of that time. There were countless nights where either Mike or I drove into downtown Kansas City at midnight to pick up Alex at a bus hub, because the northbound buses stopped operating after 7:30 pm.

By junior year, Alex was flourishing, even making the honor roll one semester. Ms. Kathy had received an e-mail from one of Alex's teachers and was eager to share it with me. Ms. Kathy prefaced the email with, *"Alex is absolutely my shining star! Watching him bloom into such a self-assured competent young adult is part of what gets me going every day! He is the epitome of why I do this job! I could not be prouder of him if he were my own and I knew that you would love this e-mail."*

Alex's teacher had written, *"My class visited the Nelson-Atkins Museum viewing room last week. I had the students break up into small groups, answer a series of questions about an object and then present their analyses to the class. Alex not only took a leadership role in his group's discussion but also volunteered to present his group's object to the class. He really did a fantastic job. This is the third course he's taken with me, and it has been such a pleasure to see him not only want to do things out of his comfort zone but also to do them so well."* Gaining confidence through his experiences was helping Alex realize his capabilities. And the positive feedback from his mentors only fueled his self-confidence and ambition.

To enhance Alex's support system, we had become acquainted with a newly established, local non-profit agency (Autism Works) that served the Autism Spectrum Disorder (ASD) community. During one of my conversations with the director, we discussed that Alex was attending art school. Since he was now advanced in his artistic knowledge, the director asked if Alex would be interested in teaching a monthly art class for youngsters on the spectrum. After talking it through with Alex he agreed to take on this volunteer project. I crafted the monthly message to promote his new art class; the director handled dissemination via a newsletter, and Alex created the class curriculum. One Saturday a month, we drove to the non-profit facility and Alex successfully taught art techniques to neurodivergent children. It was a beautiful thing to watch him interact with his students as his confidence grew.

When a new director of Autism Works took charge, she asked if the Art Institute would host the art classes on their campus, with Alex conducting the sessions. In our research to determine the viability of having non-paying students on the Institute grounds, we learned of the Art Institute's community outreach program called ArtPlay. Subsequently, Alex became an active member in the ArtPlay program and held an art class once a month on campus for autistic kiddos. The Autism Works art program continued for several months until the coordination between the Autism Works director, the autistic students, and the community outreach group became too time consuming for me to handle. Stress related to my job in sales, as well as family commitments was sucking every bit of my energy and I could not keep up with the demands of coordinating this ongoing project.

Although the program associated with Autism Works had ended, Alex continued to take part in the Art Institute's community outreach program ArtPlay. With fellow classmates, he traveled to elementary schools in poorly served areas of town where they taught art to underprivileged children. That experience gave him the confidence to dip his toes into yet another volunteer teaching position. One that did not require my coordination.

A new Medicaid-funded, arts-based day program called Imagine That! had recently been established in Kansas City. This program catered to the severely disabled who spent their days creating artwork. Again, Alex volunteered his time and talents and taught printmaking techniques once a month to the workshop attendees over a period of six months. Teaching the disabled takes additional time and energy, and Alex found himself being overwhelmed as the manager of the workshop continued to assign more and more pupils to him without any assistance. And as self-advocacy for Alex was still something he struggled to invoke, out of frustration he just walked away from the opportunity instead of asking them to reduce his workload.

With Alex's neuro disability often draining his stamina, there was no way that he would be able to hold a dedicated part time job while attending the Art Institute. It was taking every ounce of energy he had to commute, study, write, test, and create artwork into the evening hours. He spent many long days in the studio. Most mornings he left the house at 7:00 am and arrived home after a sixteen-hour day. He was assuredly pushing his limits.

With that said, it is well documented and understood that Autism is a life-long disability. Although Alex had qualified for Social Security disability at age eighteen, the state required a disability case evaluation every three years. By now, Alex was near the end of his junior year at the Art Institute. It was late spring when he received notification in the mail stating that he was due for his first three-year evaluation. The notice included a pre-established appointment date and time for Alex to meet with a psychiatrist of the state's choosing. Mike and I, as his legal guardians were not allowed to attend the appointment.

We helped Alex determine which bus would get him closest to the psychiatrist's office. When his pre-assigned appointment date arrived, he successfully navigated his way to meet with the state-appointed psychiatrist. The meeting conversation was not disclosed to us. No one shared what questions were asked. We saw no meeting notes. And of course, Alex could not recall any details related to the discussion.

He just said that the meeting went well. The entire forty-five-minute session was a mystery to us. I did not have a good feeling about the process so far.

A few weeks later, we received a notice from the state that Alex no longer qualified for Social Security disability. My mind exploded! Are you kidding me? You (Social Security) are going to determine a crucial life-affecting decision based on ONE forty-five-minute conversation? Of course, Alex was going to convey that everything was going well in his world. All his needs were being met, and his perspective was through rose-colored glasses. He was not outside looking in like the rest of us. He would happily talk about school and was rightfully proud of his accomplishments to date. Speaking casually with Alex for only a brief period, with no triggers that caused stress, anxiety, or sensory escalation, was not a fair assessment of what happened in the real world. I was incensed with the evaluation outcome!

Alex relied on his small disability income (as much as Mike and I did) to pay for his bus fare, his school cafeteria card and additional required art supplies. Alex was not encumbered with any financial burden, and he did not grasp the importance of losing his disability payments. The "denial of services" letter stated that we had the right to appeal. We researched the internet and located an attorney named Mr. G., who focused solely on Social Security Disability.

After several meetings with Mr. G., he was able to experience some of Alex's agitated behaviors brought on by a lack of social awareness and ensuing anxiety. Mike, Alex, and I sat in Mr. G's office as he explained how the Social Security appeal process would play out. The details were too much for Alex to digest and he started to zone out. When Mr. G. sternly demanded Alex's focus on the matter at hand, Alex escalated and furiously stormed out of the office. We later found him brooding outside of the building. I was infuriated that the very behaviors we worked so hard to avoid, would now have to be provoked to prove that Alex still struggled with high anxiety and a lack of social understanding caused by his neuro disability. This incident allowed Mr. G. to see that when pressure was applied to Alex, his anxiety mentally shut him down and he became overwhelmed with anger. As a result, we began to prepare for the appeal process. After six months of silence from the Social Security office, we were finally scheduled for a hearing.

The day of the appeal meeting, Mike, Alex, and I arrived at the Social Security office where we met our attorney. We were escorted to a back room where we were introduced to a senior female social security employee who conducted the appeal interview. She was very polite, with a calm demeanor. She opened the meeting with some casual conversation between her and Alex. Then, she asked me if I had any examples of Alex's behaviors related to responsibilities in the home. I said, "Alex has a small parrot named Felix. He wanted the bird so feeding and cleaning Felix's cage is supposed to be his responsibility." I relayed that I continuously had to remind him and often got negative pushback. Sometimes it would take him a week to finally change the cage liner. I continued, "More often than not, I clean the cage myself as the bird would be living in unsanitary conditions (by my standards) and I could not let it go any longer." Alex silently sat there staring at the floor and I could see in his contorted face that his anxiety was escalating. When the Social Security worker pressed Alex for a response as to why he avoided this simple chore, he snapped and with an aggravated, guttural tone he shouted, "You can just do it yourself!" Her eyes widened with the realization that the accountability of a simple task like changing a pet's cage liner caused Alex to become anxious and angry. He sat there steaming and mentally checked out for the rest of the interview.

Very little was expected of Alex related to household chores. Our family has had a housekeeper for over twenty-five years. She dusted Alex's room, changed his sheets, and scoured his bathroom. Even though Alex was taught and knew how to do his own laundry, Mike and I would handle that chore while Alex was attending school full time. Outside of his education, he had very little asked of him as we were well-aware of his sensory limitations. He was only required to succeed at school. So, asking him to clean his bird's cage liner occasionally should not have been an enormous imposition, but when asked, household chores caused him to become agitated.

A few weeks after the appeal meeting, we received a letter from Social Security stating that Alex's disability status had been reinstated. I was thoroughly disgusted with the Social Security office for making our family suffer their "dog and pony show," causing grief and undue stress over a six-month period. The entire process was unnecessary and a huge waste of everyone's time.

The last semester of Alex's Senior year at college was incredibly stressful. Not only for him, but for me as well. Unfortunately, Ms. Kathy, his special needs coordinator had retired at the end of his junior year and the school did not replace her. In my opinion, with her decades of experience and overwhelming compassion she was irreplaceable. As a result, Alex had no one-on-one support his entire senior year. While working full time, I tried to keep him on track to accomplish the lengthy list of requirements that qualified him for his degree and would allow him to graduate on time.

One of the final obligations was for each student to display their four years of studio work in a gallery setting. Most students teamed up with their friends and found a local gallery or vacant space throughout Kansas City's art district for their final presentation. Due to Alex's inability to develop and maintain friendships, he had no one to team with. As graduation was drawing near, the pressure was skyrocketing to complete this required task. With a small window of time remaining, Alex finally secured a room on the Art Institute campus where he would display his work in a solo show.

I quickly coordinated some simple refreshments consisting of cookies, nuts, and punch. I then sent a massive email to family, friends, and co-workers inviting them to the art exhibit. One extremely kind girl who was a junior in Alex's printmaking class, generously stayed late that afternoon to help with positioning his artwork on the walls and tables. Bless her heart! The two of them strategically hung oil paintings, and framed prints, and carefully positioned ceramics and glassware that Alex had designed over the last four years.

Thankfully, the show was a success. Many friends and family stopped in to support Alex during the exhibition, and appreciatively some of his prints were purchased. After initially feeling so dejected when he could not manage to be a part of his fellow classmate's presentations, his self-esteem was regained. That evening, after we packed the remaining artwork, cleaned up the refreshments and swept the floor, Mike, Alex and I, along with my mom, sisters, and Alex's volunteer friend, went out for a fun Chinese dinner to celebrate. Climbing into bed that evening, all the tension drained from my body. We had completed the last required task on the list with one week to spare before graduation.

I was not emotional at Alex's High School graduation. Honestly, I was just so relieved that he had made it through. You can imagine my surprise as I felt the tears streaming down my face at his college graduation. I was so proud of Alex's determination and hard work over the previous four years that culminated with his Bachelor of Fine Arts. There was a lot of anguish for Alex over those four years. Apparently, the struggle was worth the effort, when one day I overheard him tell a family member that attending the Kansas City Art Institute had been the best four years of his life.

# Chapter 8.  Work Life

In Missouri, the legal driving age is sixteen.  However, since Alex was emotionally a few years behind his peers, I knew he would not be mature enough to get behind the wheel of a vehicle during his high school years.  Nonetheless, at around age eighteen we thought we would give it a go.  Alex easily passed the written driver's test and obtained a permit.  Now that we were official, I eased Alex into the driver's seat and gave a rundown of the gauges, buttons, and levers.  I drove to the closest empty parking lot where we switched seats.  Becoming familiar with the feel of the car, Alex slowly began driving figure eights.  After a few weeks, we braved the public streets.  The process of physically handling the car was slow and steady, albeit my hair graying with each session.  Although Alex was able to keep the car between the lines avoiding the ditches, he struggled to grasp the subtleties of driving.

Our family went to dinner one evening and while leaving the restaurant we asked Alex if he wanted to drive home.  He agreed and got behind the wheel.  We were nose first in the parking space, which required Alex to back out.  While he physically could handle backing, he paid absolutely no attention to the people who were walking out of the restaurant.  Without turning his head, he hastily backed out of the parking space, nearly hitting the pedestrians.  Yikes!  Backup cameras with sensors did not yet exist, with what we could afford at the time, anyway.

That frightening incident was not the first time that Alex had been careless with lack of attention to his surroundings.  Accordingly, there were some heated words exchanged within our car causing Alex to emotionally spiral into irreversible shutdown mode.  He growled, "That's it, I'm not driving anymore!" He stomped out of the driver's seat, jumped into the back seat, and that was the end of him driving for the next six years.

Alex's dad had also previously taken him on a few driving outings, but it was painfully clear that neither of us had the refined skills or patience to teach driving safety to our son who lacked awareness and whose anxiety intensified under pressure. We did not know where to turn and his current case manager did not have the knowledge to assist. At this point, Alex had already attempted to pass the physical driving test and failed twice. He had completely missed a few stop signs in residential neighborhoods. A third failure would result in a lot more paperwork and additional training requirements as dictated by the state, so Alex gave up.

Now graduated from college, my twenty-two-year-old needed to find a job. Still dealing with his high anxiety and a lack of people skills, we turned to Vocational Rehabilitation Services (Voc. Rehab), a state agency that contracts with providers who assist the disabled with finding a job. After an initial meeting and completing the necessary paperwork, Voc. Rehab directed us toward a company called Vocational Services, Inc. (VSI). VSI profiled Alex's likes, dislikes, and interests. Then they researched different fields of occupation that fit Alex's criteria. Once possible employers were identified, they assisted Alex with completing a resume and coached him on the interviewing process. Then VSI helped Alex apply for employment. They even accompanied him to the interviews. The entire process took a year to complete.

Alex finally secured a part-time job with a craft and fabric retail store. During the first six months of employment, VSI provided Alex with "follow along case management" to address any questions or concerns, allowing him to integrate successfully. We were pleased with his part-time assignment as we knew that full-time would be too overwhelming in the beginning. I think back to Temple Grandin's words of wisdom imparted from her experiences as an Autistic adult. She stated, *"It is important to gradually transition from an educational setting into a career."*

Alex started his first paid job working on the store's retail floor, ensuring items were staged in their appropriate locations, answering customer's questions, and directing patrons as appropriate. "Where's the restroom?" was a common request. He got along well with his fellow coworkers. However, in the beginning, before he became fully familiar with the store layout, the cranky old-lady shoppers were mean to him when he could not answer a question to their liking, calling him "stupid." Eventually, Alex landed a position in the fabrics department where he restocked bolts of fabric that had been cut, as well as stocked new fabric that arrived.

Within two years he was periodically assisting in the custom framing department. He thrived there, enjoying the creativity of helping a customer select the appropriate frame and matting, and then assembling the project. After three years of part-time commitment to this craft store, things were going well for Alex. That is until the manager developed some serious health problems and had to retire. A new manager was hired and that is when things went downhill. She cut Alex's schedule from twenty-eight hours to a measly five hours per week. That crushed his self-esteem. When a full-time position in framing became available Alex applied but wasn't accepted. The new manager hired someone from the outside and Alex had to train the new hire to use the point-of-sale system to document the specifics of the framing project. Alex was highly disappointed but continued to work his greatly reduced hours in fabrics.

One day I was shopping for fabric in Alex's place of employment. Having selected my material, I ambled over to the cutting counter. Alex was behind the counter, as was the new manager. Alex and I were conversing in our own unique dialogue while the manager listened in. Not understanding Alex's sense of humor, the manager made a snide comment to me about Alex. I do not know why she felt compelled to disrespect Alex, because I was in no way showing body language that suggested I was a displeased customer. At that point she had no idea that I was his mother, and it became painfully clear to me that she did not have the skills to tolerate the uniqueness of my son's personality. Nor did she possess the requisite leadership skills to manage someone's strengths and weaknesses. Alex was miserable working for her and concluded that now was the right time to start looking for another job. I've often heard that people do not leave a job because of the work, they leave because of poor management. From my perspective, that certainly applied to this case.

During most of the three years working for the fabric store Alex rode the public bus when he could, but Mike and I drove him on weekends when the bus schedules were reduced. That limited our freedom to travel or go out on the weekends, as we always had to be available to chauffeur on Friday and Saturday evenings. We could not rely on Uber as those drivers were kept busy in densely populated night-life areas of the city, and the facility where Alex worked was a residential-rural location.

Finally, when Alex was twenty-five and still working at the fabric store his new disabilities case manager informed us of a rehabilitation center in Kansas City (now called Ability). We learned that this certified Comprehensive Outpatient Rehabilitation Center provided driving lessons to people with special needs. Hallelujah! I remember feeling immensely hopeful that Alex would gain his independence and Mike and I would recapture a bit of our social lives.

I immediately called the rehab organization to determine what was needed to schedule an evaluation appointment for Alex. After submitting the necessary paperwork, which included a doctor's release stating that Alex had no history of seizures, I received a call to confirm that Alex was approved to begin the process. Within a month we were at the rehab facility where they assessed Alex's cognitive, visual, and motor skills. He was able to demonstrate physical driving ability, and as a result they were confident that he would be safely driving with only thirty hours of instruction. Training classes focused on:

- Decrease anxiety when driving – start with residential, progressing to commercial, then highway traffic.

- Improve functional visual scanning for traffic signs, pedestrians, and road hazards and how to respond to each.

- Preparation for behind the wheel evaluation at the DMV including parallel parking and parking/backing up in crowded lots.

- Improve lane changes in commercial and highway traffic by providing easy to remember steps - practice from less traveled areas to more congested.

- Provide calming strategies while driving.

I could not fathom how this agency would improve his visual scanning to keep him from blowing through stop signs and learned that the driving instructor used a technique termed "commentary driving" where Alex verbally called out every traffic sign as he saw them.

After several months of instruction and intense practice, the rehab center deemed Alex capable of driving. The moment of truth was upon us as we drove Alex to the driver's license testing facility and apprehensively waited for him to return in our car. This was Alex's third driving attempt at a driver's license, and we were ecstatic when he returned and exclaimed that he had successfully passed! Woohoo! Having a license would open a whole new world of independence for him and we could not have been more pleased.

At this point, Alex was still employed by the craft and fabric store making eight dollars an hour and working only five hours a week. It was clear to Alex that he had no future with this company. He attempted to find another job on his own and was successful at landing a few, but each lasted only a day. He enjoyed screen-printing in college and obtained employment with a small, family-owned T-shirt printing company. After one day on the job, he realized that production numbers and extreme accuracy were key performance indicators, which caused his anxiety to rise. The company provided no feedback at the end of the day. Alex had no idea if he did well or if they were disappointed in his performance, therefore he could not bring himself to return the next day.

This reminded me of valuable advice given by Mike Hardwick, founder of Churchill Mortgage, in his book "Keep Chopping Wood" – *"No matter what level a person is in business, from an entry level worker to a CEO, the need to have guidance and support is a crucial element in giving people the confidence and purpose to achieve their dreams."* This small T-shirt company fell short in providing the guidance Alex desperately needed to feel that his contribution was sufficient to remain in their employment.

After a few weeks of ongoing interviews, Alex was employed by yet another small, family-owned apparel facility that screen-printed T-shirts. After the first day of enforced production, with no lunch or rest breaks, and Alex's lack of self-advocacy he was completely famished and wiped out at the end of his eight-hour day. According to Missouri and Kansas state labor laws, with few exceptions, the law does not require employers to provide meal or rest breaks. I find that to be abusive and unkind. How can a business owner expect employees to work with maximum effectiveness and sustain physical well-being without refueling? I was glad that Alex did not want to return.

Finding a decent job on his own was not proving beneficial, although I was pleased with his determination. Despite his efforts, we revisited with Vocational Rehabilitation Services. This time we used the state-contracted agency named Ability. This was the same agency that victoriously provided Alex with driving lessons. Within a month Alex was successfully hired by the Nelson Atkins Museum of Art, a must visit if you are in Kansas City, MO. We were thrilled! It was a perfect fit to be surrounded by precious art in a mostly non-chaotic and quiet environment. His position was part-time in security as an attendant in the galleries, ensuring that artifacts were not touched, that backpacks were positioned on the front of the body (so as not to unwittingly damage valuables), and again, answering the question, "Where is the restroom?"

Alex worked part-time as a gallery usher with the museum for three years, until he accepted a full-time assignment escorting and assisting contractors that provided maintenance services to the museum structure. The duties of this role carried a little more responsibility and gave Alex a sense of ownership and accomplishment. With full-time pay, Alex was now triumphantly able to say "good-bye" to his Social Security disability stipend. A major milestone worthy of celebration.

After another year passed, Alex applied for and accepted a promotion with full benefits, working with the museum's event setup team. At the time I am writing this narrative, it remains his current position. And recently, a handful of Alex's colleagues formed a band where Alex is playing bass guitar. Watching him come out of his shell and doing the things that he loves is pure joy for me. Now working toward completing his fifth year, the Nelson Atkins Museum of Art has been a kind and generous employer. A true gem to the heartbeat of Kansas City.

# Chapter 9. The Journey Continues

Having a neurodiverse child has enabled me to grow in ways that I could never have imagined. I was born in New Jersey and raised in a catholic school until age fourteen, where each day for nine long years, an hour of religious instruction was doled out. Additionally, I attended mass every Wednesday and Sunday. You may think that bestowing so much holiness upon a child would ensure that they possessed a kind and nurturing soul. Not so. During my early adolescent years, us neighborhood kids would hang out every morning on the side of a busy two-lane road while waiting for our school bus. Each day, a small, yellow bus would whiz by, carrying children that we did not recognize. I remember spouting one day, "There goes the tard-cart." A callous statement, spoken by an immature and compassionless child. Somehow, I missed the persistently imparted godly messages. I can only assume that because of my hard nature the divine Father granted me a special needs child. I guess the Lord thought, "Geez, if incessant religion isn't going to turn her, then I'll have to find some other way."

As a result, I am appreciative for a broader, more accepting view of the world. I attribute that open-mindedness to rearing a child that required perseverance, patience, and unfettered acceptance. I understand that we are all wired differently. Tolerance and unconditional love are necessary components for our children to flourish. The journey has not been easy, but well worth the effort.

I am grateful for the ability to relish and celebrate the small, as well as large milestones. From speaking the word "mommy" for the first time at age 4; to mastering potty training at the age of 5; to sticking with the violin through 12th grade; to graduating with a BFA from the KC Art Institute; to obtaining a driver's license at age 25; and successfully holding down a full-time job. All these accomplishments seemed dreadfully out of reach when first given the diagnosis of Autism. As each milestone was achieved, a sense of perpetual motion provided hope, fueling the next challenge.

At age thirty, Alex still lives at home. Currently, he and his "life coach" are working through the process of finding a suitable and affordable apartment so that Alex can learn to live on his own and become further engaged in his community. We look forward to arriving at this next milestone in his life.

Surprisingly, in April 2022, Alex attended his 10-year high school class reunion – delayed two years due to the COVID pandemic. From a class of over 400 students, only fifteen people attended the cozy, local venue. The small showing was most likely a benefit for Alex, with less sensory input. He spoke with seven classmates that evening. Standing in our kitchen, he expressed that he had a good time, and I could see his confident and uplifted enthusiasm as he recalled his conversations. I was impressed with his bravery, as he previously had no interest in large social gatherings due to anxiety.

Autism Spectrum Disorder (ASD) is presented with such a wide variety of characteristics, abilities, disabilities, and levels of severity. Our story is not intended to be a "how to" guide. Each family with an exceptional child will experience their own unique journey. For Alex, he will have an assigned Case Manager for the remainder of his life, who will oversee his annually reviewed, individualized service plan documenting his interests, talents, likes, dislikes, needs, and goals.

I cannot express earnestly enough that early intervention for a child with a disability is crucial for them to achieve their greatest potential. I cringe when I think about where Alex would be without the boundless support that he, and our family received since he was first diagnosed at age two and a half. Society's investment in Alex's early years has minimized the supports that are needed in his adult life. He progressed from a non-verbal, non-compliant toddler to a productive adult, earning a living and contributing to society. There are not enough words to quantify the positive effects on humanity that values diversity and provides resources to the special needs community. For that I am eternally grateful.

I will end with a quote from Mike Hardwick that I think encompasses the journey of raising a child with a disability. *"It's important to know that progress, not perfection, can go a long way toward helping someone realize their potential."*

# INDEX

1. Ability KC -  Page 118

In 1947 two local organizations, Children's Therapeutic Learning Center and Rehabilitation Institute of Kansas City, opened their doors to serve children and adults with disabilities. Seventy years later those organizations came together as one, Ability KC.  Our mission is to build brighter futures for children and adults with disabilities by providing comprehensive educational, vocational, and therapeutic services.

2. Alex J Krahenbuhl Studios - Pages 129-161

Facebook page that highlights Alex's artwork.

3. Autism Works - Page 109

Autism Works Inc is a non-profit organization where dedicated parents, volunteers and staff come together to bring support and programs to families whose lives are affected by Autism Spectrum Disorders (ASD).

## 4. Circle of Friends - Page 82

ABOUT | circleofriends

Circle of Friends (CoF) is a social and language skills program that provides valuable support to students with special needs. CoF provides support and strategies for educators to create opportunities for socially isolated students that reduce isolation and increase connection.

## 5. Early Childhood Education - Page 25

Early Education / Homepage (nkcschools.org)

NKC Schools is proud to offer a variety of Early Education programs to meet the needs of our community. All our programs provide opportunities for exploration, discovery, creativity, problem solving, and social interaction.

## 6. First Steps - Page 18

First Steps | dmh.mo.gov

First Steps offers coordinated services and assistance to young children with special needs and their families. First Steps is designed for children, birth to age three, who have delayed development or diagnosed conditions that are associated with developmental disabilities. First Steps is a collaborative effort of four state agencies - the Departments of Elementary and Secondary Education, Health, Mental Health, and Social Services. First Steps is supported through federal and state dollars, public and private insurance reimbursement, and family cost participation.

## 7. Imagine That! - Page 110

Imagine That! (imaginethatkc.org)

An arts-based day program for creative individuals with developmental disabilities.

8. Kansas City Regional Offices (KCRO) – Missouri Department of Mental Health - Page 10

Kansas City Regional Offices | dmh.mo.gov

The Missouri Division of Developmental Disabilities provides services for individuals with developmental disabilities such as intellectual disabilities, cerebral palsy, Down syndrome, autism, and epilepsy.

9. "Keep Chopping Wood" – Mike Hardwick - Page 120

Mike Hardwick - President and CEO - Churchill Mortgage Corporation | LinkedIn

"Keep Chopping Wood" is an engaging and inspirational book that tells the colorful life story of Lawson H. Hardwick, III, one of the most well-known businessmen and philanthropists in Nashville, Tennessee and around the country.

10. Northwest Missouri Autism Project - Page 23

Northwest Missouri Autism Project | dmh.mo.gov

The Northwest Missouri Autism Project (NWMAP) serves individuals in 20 counties throughout northwestern Missouri. In order to be eligible for Autism Project services, individuals must be eligible to receive services from the Division of Developmental Disabilities and have a diagnosis of autism spectrum disorder.

11. Special Needs Planning Center - Page 100

Home - Special Needs Planning Center at CommunityAmericaSpecial Needs Planning Center at CommunityAmerica (snpcenter.com)

The Special Needs Planning Center was formed specifically to work with families who have children with special needs. The firm was created out of the need for a comprehensive planning service which would assist families in coordinating their legal and financial planning with the intent of preserving government benefits such as Social Security.

## 12. "The Moment of Lift" – Melinda French Gates - Page 83

The Moment of Lift Summary and Study Guide | SuperSummary

"The Moment of Lift" is a moving memoir by Melinda Gates talking about her work for the last twenty years in heading the foundation founded by her and her ex-husband Bill Gates.

## 13. Vocational Rehabilitation Services - Page 116

State Vocational Rehabilitation Agencies | Rehabilitation Services Administration (ed.gov)

Rehabilitation Services Administration provides formula grants to Vocational Rehabilitation (VR) agencies to administer the State VR Services, State Supported Employment Services, and Independent Living Services for Older Individuals Who Are Blind programs in all 50 states, the District of Columbia, Puerto Rico, and four Territories.

## 14. Vocational Services Inc. (VSI) - Page 116

vsiserve.org/contact.html

Nationally accredited and state certified, VSI has been providing employment and other services for people with disabilities for over 50 years – and serving the business community with on-demand, flexible services, and programs.

**Peter Green,**
Ink and Watercolor
on Paper

**J. B. Lenoir,**
Mixed Media on
Canvas

**Soldiers in Slings,** Ink on Paper

**Ornament,**
Ink on Paper

**Ripened Pumpkin,**
Ink on Paper

**Snow,**
Ink on Paper

**Tread,**
Ink on Paper

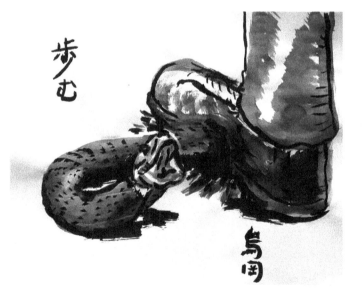

**Overgrown,**
Ink on Paper

**Ancient Bust of Senusret III,**
Ink on Paper

**G-S-S-1,**
Oil on Glass

**W-S-S-1,**
Oil on Glass

**C-S-S-1,**
Oil on Glass

**T-S-S-1,**
Oil on Glass

**G-P-S-S-1,**
Oil on Glass

**H-S-S-1,**
Oil on Glass

**Along the Castle Walls,**
Ink and Gouache on Postcard

**Am I Shallow?**
Gouache on Paper

**Calavera Apache,** Ink, Gouache, and Oil on Cardboard

**Dangers of the Mountains,** Ink and Gouache on Paper

**The End of the Pain,** Ink, Gouache, and Watercolor on Cardboard

**Train Depot, Eureka Springs, AR,**
Watercolor on Paper

**North Doors at the
Nelson Atkins Museum,**
Watercolor over Silverpoint on Paper

**El Que le Canto a San Pedro no le Volvera a Cantar,** Digital Art

**El Diablito,** Digital Art

**Red Mill of Alley Spring, Missouri,** Black and White Charcoal on Toned Paper

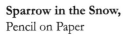

**Sparrow in the Snow,**
Pencil on Paper

**Linn Branch Creek Bridge at English Landing Park,**
Black and White Charcoal on Toned Paper

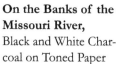

**On the Banks of the Missouri River,**
Black and White Charcoal on Toned Paper

**Lakewood in the Afternoon,** Black and White Charcoal on Toned Paper

**Jorma Kaukonen, Hot Tuna,**
Black and White Charcoal on
Toned Paper

**Marriage of Saint Catherine
After Alessandro Magnasco,**
Black and White Charcoal on-
Toned Paper

**Pearl, The Neighborhood Cat,**
Ink and Watercolor on Glass

**Irises,**
Ink on Paper

**Busking on
Departure at
Union Station,**
Oil on Canvas

**Couldn't Get Out of
Hodge Jail,**
Watercolor on Paper

**City Lake, Lawson, Missouri,** Watercolor on Glass

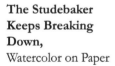

**The Studebaker Keeps Breaking Down,** Watercolor on Paper

**Sunset Overlook, Ha
Ha Tonka, Missouri,**
Oil on Glass

**Whitetail Trail, Parkville,
Missouri,**
Ink and Watercolor on Glass

**Roses Over the Fence,** Ink on Paper

**Racing in Osborn,** Ink and Watercolor on Glass

**Sunrise on the Missouri River,** Watercolor on Glass

**Gokoku-Ji Pagoda after Tomikichiro Tokuriki,** Digital Art

**Battleground of Pea Ridge, Arkansas,** Gouache and Oil on Canvas

**The Encounter of
Kagutsuchi,**
Ink and Gouache on Paper

**Resting at the Trenches,**
Oil on Glass

**The Cellist,**
Ink and Gouache on Paper

**Sam Chatmon,**
Ink on Paper

**Alvin Youngblood Hart,**
Ink on Paper

**Mississippi John Hurt,**
Ink on Paper

**Lightnin' Hopkins,**
Ink on Paper

**Robert Johnson,**
Ink on Paper

**Albert King,**
Ink on Paper

**Rory Gallagher,**
Ink on Paper

**David "Honeyboy" Edwards,**
Ink on Paper

**Fats Domino,**
Ink on Paper

**Roosevelt Sykes,**
Ink on Paper

**In the Cold Night,** Etching and Aquatint on Paper

**After the Flood,** Etching and Aquatint on Paper

**Self-Portrait,** Oil on Glass

# Acknowledgments

A huge debt of gratitude goes out to all the North Kansas City School District teachers and administration that supported Alex from early education to graduation. There are too many to name over the fifteen-year span, but special thanks go to Christine Murray, Tammy Bunch, Julia Wesley, and Ryan Fuger. Your tireless efforts were the catalyst for Alex's success. You will always remain in my heart for your resolute devotion to your profession.

Ms. Kathy Keller, without you, Alex would not have successfully navigated his way through college. Your commitment to the students at KCAI was unrivaled.

My continued appreciation to David Schupp of Behavioral Innovations. He has been a rock for Alex, playing many roles in his success related to community integration.

An enormous thank you goes to Scott Colbert, Alletta Dickson, and Rachelle Henningsen for reviewing my manuscript and providing detailed and constructive comments.

Finally, my heartfelt admiration to my husband Mike, our sons Alex and Austin, as well as our extended family, for their unwavering support. I am truly blessed and grateful for each of you.

# About the Author

Theresa Krahenbuhl lives in Kansas City, MO, with her husband Mike and two sons, Alex and Austin. She worked for the Postal Service for 34 years, retiring in 2018. She is most content when traveling throughout the United States in her camper, leisurely hiking the picturesque state and national park trails. When at home, she volunteers with Harvester's - Community Food Network, relishes time with her extended family, enjoys live music, theater, sewing, reading and outings with friends.

Printed in the USA
CPSIA information can be obtained
at www.ICGtesting.com
LVHW050230040124
767839LV00042B/1216